LEMONS & LIMES

Super Citrus Fruits
& Their Health Benefits

LEMONS
&LIMES

Super Citrus Fruits
& Their Health Benefits

Margaret Briggs

Abbeydale Press

ISBN 978-1-86147-239-7

1 3 5 7 9 10 8 6 4 2

Published by Abbeydale Press
an imprint of Bookmart Ltd
Registered number 2372865
Trading as Bookmart Ltd
Blaby Road, Wigston, Leicester
LE18 4SE, England

Produced by Omnipress Limited, UK
Illustrations by Tegan Sharrard
Cover design by Omnipress Limited

Printed in Dubai

ABOUT THE AUTHOR

Margaret Briggs was a teacher for 30 years, working in Kent, Germany, North Yorkshire and Sussex.

Since leaving teaching she has had more time for gardening and cooking and has embarked on a second career as a freelance writer, researcher and editor, alongside her writer husband, Lol. Six years ago the couple bought a dilapidated house in south-west France. The house is now restored and Margaret and Lol divide their time between Sussex and the Gironde, with two contrasting gardens to develop.

Margaret has written other books in this series: *Vinegar — 1001 Practical Uses, Gardening Hints and Tips, Porridge — Oats and their Many Uses, Honey — and its Many Health Benefits, Beetroot — The Vitality Plant & its Medicinal Benefits, Bicarbonate of Soda — A Very Versatile Natural Substance* and *Garlic & Onions — The Many Uses & Medicinal Benefits.*

CONTENTS

Introduction   7

Where Do Lemons, Citrons & Limes
      Come From?   9

The History Behind Lemons & Limes   39

Nutrition And Health Benefits   53

Industrial Uses   71

Beauty Treatments   85

      Natural Ingredient Facials   87

      Other Treatments   94

      Hair Treatments   98

Cleaning With Lemons   101

Cooking With Lemons & Limes   111

      Drinks With Lemons & Limes   115

      Salads And Starters   126

      Main Dishes With Lemons & Limes   134

      Desserts   141

      Cakes And Biscuits   151

      Preserves And Pickles   155

Introduction

Can you think of a fruit which you can put into a gin and tonic, use to flavour the salad dressing, the main course or the dessert and then use to help with the washing up afterwards? Oh, and polish the copper pans with as well, and remove stains from the tablecloth at the end of the meal? Only the lemon can achieve all of these. Its close cousin the lime will do nearly as well, although it may not spring to mind as readily.

The great thing about lemons and limes is that they smell wonderful when you cut them and somehow they promote a feel-good, clean, fresh zing factor about the place, rather like the smell of coffee or fresh toast first thing in the morning. Lemons and limes not only smell good, however, and add considerably to a whole range of culinary dishes: they really are good for you! You don't have to justify using them all the time on health grounds either, because they are packed with vitamins and nutrients which can actually prevent or ease some medical conditions.

Lemons and limes boast quite a history through the ages, with some interesting cultural uses as well. Despite some of the more eye-watering uses contrived over the years, they have saved many a sailor from scurvy. Gandhi apparently ate lemons every day and he believed in eating only what your body needs. You are what you eat and drink. So why not add a little zest to your life?

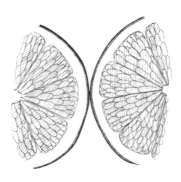

Where Do Lemons, Citrons & Limes Come From?

Lemons, limes and citrons all belong to the same family and broadly enjoy the same conditions, although limes are widely grown in tropical and subtropical areas. Most lemons come from Italy and the USA and the main lime-producing countries are Mexico, Brazil and the USA. Citrons, often bought as lemons, are mainly grown for processing and for religious needs.

TASTY FAMILY TREE

Lemons (*Citrus limon*) and limes (*Citrus aurantifolia*) are plants belonging to the *Rutaceae* family. This family of plants includes those with edible fruits and hardwood timber. Other trees include the mahogany, mango, cashew nut, frankincense and myrrh. They are usually pollinated by insects, including small flies and bees, and produce fragrant flowers, conspicuous for their colour.

The lemon is a small tree which can grow to anything between 3 m and 6 m (10–20 feet). There are about 50 varieties which have developed throughout the centuries of its cultivation. Other members of the citrus family include the bergamot, which is closely related, as well as the following:

- Grapefruit (*C. paradisii*)
- Mandarin orange (*C. nobilis deliciosa*)
- Shaddock or Pummelo (*C. maxima*)
- Sour orange (*C. Aurantium*)
- Sweet orange (*C. sinensis*)

The kumquat (*Fortunella*) and trifoliate orange (*Poncirus*) are also included under the common name citrus, although they do not belong to the botanical group *Citrus*. However, since this book is about lemons and limes, we'll forget about the above for now.

The name *Limonum* comes from the Arabic *Limun* or *Limu*, which probably comes from the Sanskrit *Nimbuka*. The principal species of citrus fruits are lemons, limes and citron or cedrat. Citron or *Citrus medica* is a group of varieties which differ in the size and shape of the fruit.

LEMON (CITRUS LIMONIA)

TREE

This is a small, widely branched tree that grows 10 to 20 feet high. It is thorny and evergreen. The leaves are narrow, ovate and light green, and there are sharp spines in the axils of the stalks. The irregularly arranged branches and bark vary in colour from grey to green on younger branches and twigs may be purplish.

FLOWERS

The flower buds appear in pairs or on their own in leaf axils and are tinted with purplish pink. The five petals are white inside and purple on the outer surface. Dried flowers and leaves are used in pharmacy in France. The flowers have both male and female organs and reproduce by seeds formed without sexual fusion, so are self-fertilising.

FRUIT

The egg-shaped yellow fruit is usually pointed at both ends and the fairly smooth skin or peel (epicarp) is dented with oil glands. This outer layer can vary a great deal in thickness and has a fragrant smell but bitter taste.

The peel is white and spongy on the inside and is called the mesocarp or albedo. It is nearly tasteless but is the main source of commercial pectin. The light-coloured flesh has thin juice sacks or segments. The seeds or pips are ovoid and smooth, although some seedless varieties have been developed.

Lemons are grown for their acidic juice, used extensively in flavouring and in making various drinks. The juice is pressed fresh for pharmaceutical purposes, the amount of citric acid being greatest in December to January and least in August. Sometimes the peel is candied. You can read more about that later on.

COMMERCIAL CULTIVATION

Lemon trees are grown extensively in Mediterranean countries on a commercial basis and they are also grown as pot plants and as outdoor shrubs in regions fairly free from frost. They are also grown commercially in California. The botanist Linnaeus named the lemon tree as a variety of the citron, but *C. limonia* is much more widely grown than the citron. The roots and wood are cut in winter. Lemon wood is attractive and takes a beautiful polish.

Trees for commercial planting can be grown from seed but are usually propagated by budding or grafting the chosen variety onto rootstock of other citrus species, such as the grapefruit or a type of orange. This prevents some diseases spreading on rootstocks which are more uniform and less susceptible to disease. Propagation takes place when the buds are in growth, often between March and May. An alternative form of producing new plants is by layering. A branch is covered in plastic and sunk into the soil where it will develop roots.

Young trees can bear fruit after about three years and after five years may be producing commercial crops. They reach full maturity after about 15 years and may live for 80 years. The average tree will produce 1,500 lemons each year. Trees are usually cut back severely after 12 years, or replaced. Weeds must be controlled but lemon trees are very sensitive to herbicides.

Trees are grown in orchards or groves, spaced around 5–8 m (16–26 feet) apart. Lemon trees bloom throughout the year and the fruit may be picked from 6 to 10 times each year, usually while still green. It may be kept after curing for up to three months.

PESTS AND DISEASES
Phoma tracheiphila is a fungal disease affecting all citrus species in the Mediterranean and Black Sea areas as well as Asia, North Africa and South America. It is spread through wounds to the wood during hard winters, causing die-back of twigs and branches in spring. It reduces the quantity and quality of lemons produced. Lemon trees can be attacked by various viruses. Control may be achieved by careful pruning and burning of diseased branches to allow better aeration.

CLIMATE AND SOIL

The best Mediterranean environment to grow lemon trees is, as my geography teacher once made us learn, warm wet winters, hot dry summers, plenty of sunshine throughout the year and very little frost. When rain is concentrated in autumn and winter, irrigation is necessary for the citrus plants, which cannot stand long dry spells in summer.

Citrus trees are tolerant of a range of soils. Those in California and Sicily are somewhat rich in volcanic minerals. Excellent growth is maintained on loam and clay soils, which have good drainage. The pH should be between 5.5 and 6.5.

Lemon trees have a relatively limited climatic range. Because of its more or less continuous growth, the lemon is more sensitive to cold than oranges and grapefruits. It recovers less well from injury caused by cold snaps. Temperatures below freezing will seriously damage the wood unless there has been a cold fortnight preceding freezing temperatures, when the growth will have slowed down. Flowers and young fruit are killed at -1°C (29°F).

Lemons like the climate of coastal areas such as southern Italy or California, where the changes in temperature in winter months are less pronounced than inland. Strangely enough, these areas are also too cool in summer for proper ripening of oranges and grapefruit.

HARVESTING

Picking lemons must be done by hand. The fruits are highly prone to oil spotting (oleocellosis) and cannot be handled roughly or picked wet. Italian lemons for export are harvested as early as possible and are cured naturally in transit. American producers have adopted the practices of picking at any time after the fruits reach a 25% juice content, and using rings to gauge the commercially acceptable size, of between 5.4 cm and 6.25 cm (2⅛–2½ inches). Some producers have found this practice too costly and harvest the entire crop at one time. They grade for fresh sale or processing in the packing-house and discard all undersized fruits. Shame!

Once sorted according to colour, the lemons are washed to rid them of any bacteria and possible contamination from the surface of the peel. They are then coated with a fungicide and a thin layer of wax. In this way they are cured and stored until ready for shipping or processing.

Lemons are harvested all year round with peaks in May, June and August. In Italy the seasons are defined as follows:

The autumn and the winter lemons (*primofiore*) have the best quality, but the two main productions are the *bianchetti* and the *verdelli*.

• *PRIMOFIORE*

The main blossoms last from March to June, producing lemons cropped from September to October. Autumn or winter lemons are cropped from November to May. Winter lemons have a rougher peel or epicarp and a greater sourness.

• *BIANCHETTI*

The second wave of blossoms lasts from June to the end of July: it produces lemons which are cropped from February to May. *Bianchetti* are lighter yellow and have a lower level of sourness.

• *VERDELLI*

In Sicily, growers have made a practice of withholding water in summer for a month or two until the trees begin to wilt. They are then irrigated and given high nitrogen fertiliser. This produces a second bloom in August or early September and a crop the following summer, when lemons are scarce and prices are high. This system is called the *Verdelli* process.

The third blossoming, forced if necessary, lasts from August to October: at the end of April it produces the *maggiolini* and from May to September the *verdelli* and the *bastardi*. *Verdelli*, which ripen in the summer of the following year, are cheaper. The *verdelli* have a smoother epicarp, a low sourness and almost no pips. The *bastardi* ripen after a year or so and have a smooth epicarp and a deep yellow colour.

VARIETIES OF LEMONS

There are nearly 50 identified varieties of lemons growing around the world. The two basic types are acid and sweet. The acid types are dominated by two varieties, the large Eureka and the smooth-skinned Lisbon. These cultivars are not grown widely in the Mediterranean countries, in particular in Italy, because they are very susceptible to the *Phoma tracheiphila* fungus.

ITALIAN VARIETIES

A number of varieties are grown in Italy, but the most common is *Femminello comune*, also called oval *Femminello* or *Ruvittaru*, accounting for about 70% of Italian lemons.

FEMMINELLO COMUNE / FEMMINELLO OVALE

This is the leading cultivar in Italy, accounting for around 75% of the total lemon production. Twenty per cent of the crop is processed as juice. One of the oldest Italian varieties, it is short-elliptic with a low, blunt nipple or point and rounded at the base. It is medium-sized, has about 10 segments and is tender, aromatic, juicy and very acidic. It fruits all year but mainly in late winter and spring. The tree is almost thornless, medium-to-very-vigorous, but susceptible to disease. At present it is principally cultivated in Sicily and in Calabria. This cultivar, grown in Sicily since ancient times, was the originator of various local cultivars, including *Santa Teresa*, *Incappucciato* and *Sfusato di Favazzina*, all of which can tolerate disease. *Femminello comune* has five annual flowerings, to which five different names of fruit harvests correspond.

FEMMINELLO LUNARIO

This cultivar has a smaller content of citric acid and essential oils, compared to *Femminello comune*. Thanks to its capacity to produce flowers and fruit all the year round, it can often be found in kitchen gardens and gardens, and it is surely the most common cultivar used to produce ornamental vase plants.

SFUSATO AMALFITANO (OR *FEMMINELLO SFUSATO*)

This local cultivar of uncertain origin grows in the

particular microclimate between the Lattari range of mountains and the southern slope of the coast of Amalfi. The fruit is practically pipless and of elongated shape. Sensitive to the winds and to the infections of *Phoma tracheiphila*, it has an average yield. It is larger than lemons from the other Mediterranean areas, it can be preserved for a longer time and its peel is thicker and rougher. About 100 years ago farmers on the coast of Amalfi produced the first lemon liqueur, *Limoncello*, from this variety.

INTERDONATO
This variety is probably a hybrid from Messina in Sicily, dating from 1875. It has a good resistance to the *Phoma tracheiphila* fungus. The plant is not very productive, but ripens early, allowing a good production of the *Primofiore* (September–October) for marketing. The fruit is quite large and the juice is very acidic, though not abundant.

MONACHELLO
Very tolerant to *Phoma tracheiphila*, but the plants are not very productive, so it is necessary to use forcing methods. This type is not so acidic and has been grown throughout Italy.

OTHER IMPORTANT VARIETIES
EUREKA
This is probably the most widely grown lemon variety in the world. It is the most common variety in America and is also grown in Spain. Its disadvantage is that it doesn't tolerate low temperatures well. It is a bitter lemon with a high juice and acid content. The fruit should be thin-skinned and virtually seedless.

Eureka originated from seed taken from an Italian lemon, planted in Los Angeles in 1858; the fruit is elliptic to oblong, with a moderately protruding nipple at the apex and a low collar at the base. It bears fruit all year round, but mostly in late winter, spring and early summer when the demand for lemons is high. It is grown commercially in Israel, California and Australia, where it accounts for around half of the lemon plantings.

Eureka SL from South Africa is totally seedless and has a higher rind oil content. It is a more rounded fruit than the original Eureka and is therefore less acceptable to the Japanese, for whom the shape is particularly important.

LISBON

The Lisbon lemon is a good quality bitter lemon with a bright yellow colour, good texture, high juice and acid levels and thin skin. Lisbon trees, probably originating in Portugal, can be more vigorous than Eureka and are very thorny, particularly as young trees. Fruit tends to be borne inside the tree canopy where it receives some protection from wind and sun. This variety is very common in Florida and is also grown commercially in California, where it arrived from Australia, the land of its first introduction in 1824. It tolerates low temperatures much better than Eureka. In India it is low-yielding and short-lived.

VILLAFRANCA

This variety was cloned from Eureka. It is one of the most common varieties in Spain and is also widely grown in Florida. It was imported from the Mediterranean around 1875. It is a strong, productive plant which produces medium-sized fruit with many pips. The juice is sour and aromatic.

GENOA (GENOVA)

Introduced into California from Genoa in 1875, this variety has similar characteristics to Eureka. It is grown commercially in regions of India, Chile and Argentina, where it is appreciated for its vigorous growth, resistance to cold and dense foliage. In Chile it accounts for over 80% of the planted area. Genoa produces fruit almost all year round. The fruit is ellipsoid in shape with a small pointed neck and nipple and is of medium size. It has a smooth thin rind, high juice content and a relatively low number of seeds. It bears fruit on the outside of the canopy, making it prone to wind damage.

FINO
This winter-producing variety is a Lisbon type lemon. It is thorny and vigorous, with fruit produced abundantly. Fino is planted extensively in the Murcia area of Spain and is noted for its smooth rind texture and consistent heavy crops. The main crop is produced in winter and it yields more fruit than Eureka. Recently it has been introduced to Australia.

MEYER
Citrus meyeri, or Lemon Meyer, is not a true lemon but a natural hybrid of the lemon (*Citrus limon*) and the sweet orange (*Citrus sinensis*). It comes from near Beijing in China, where it was discovered by Frank Meyer in 1908. The fruit is very similar to the common lemon, although it is both less sour and juicier. This species, appreciated also for its good resistance to temperatures, is one of the most used for ornamental purposes. While not a true lemon, its fruit are used as a lemon substitute despite being much less acid than true lemons. The tree is spreading and relatively small, nearly thornless and more cold tolerant than true lemons. It is popular in south Texas, where Meyer lemons are known locally as Valley lemons. Elsewhere it is popular as a garden fruit tree, as it is quite prolific. Fruit is borne throughout much of the year, and in the tropical climate of Northern Australia trees produce fruit more or less year-round.

BABOON
This oval variety with a tapered neck originated in Brazil. It has an intense yellow colour to both its rind and heavily seeded flesh. It is also highly acidic, with a tart taste that is more like the lime.

BERNA or BERNIA, VEMA, VERNIA
This, the leading cultivar of Spain is also important in Algeria and Morocco. Trees are vigorous, large and prolific, producing elongated, rough-textured lemons which ripen mostly in winter. Fruits keep well on the tree until summer, but may become too large. This variety has recently been introduced to Australia

LIMONIERA 8A

This is currently the preferred selection in California, Arizona and Argentina. It has similar vigour to Eureka but blossoms more, leading to a much longer harvesting period. In Arizona it is picked twice a month from April to October and once a month from November to March. It has a high rind oil yield.

BEARSS

This variety came originally from Sicily in 1892 and was discovered in a grove in Florida, in 1952. It closely resembles Lisbon but is highly susceptible to scab and oil spotting. Nevertheless, it has been propagated commercially since 1953 because the peel is rich in oil. It constitutes 20% of Brazil's lemon and lime crop.

NEPALI OBLONG (ASSAM or PAT NEBU)

This lemon originated in Assam. The fruit resembles a citron in some aspects, being long-elliptic with a wide, short nipple. The peel is greenish-yellow, smooth, glossy and medium-thick. The pulp is also greenish-yellow, in 11 segments, fine-grained, very juicy, of medium acidity, with few or no seeds. The tree is large, vigorous, spreading, medium-thorny and prolific. It is grown commercially in India.

NEPALI ROUND

This is of Indian origin. The fruit is round, without a distinct nipple, juicy and seedless. The tree is large, vigorous, compact and nearly thornless. It is successfully cultivated in Southern India.

HARVEY

This variety was found by Harvey Smith on a property in Florida. The fruit is much like Eureka. The tree is highly tolerant of the cold and compatible with several root-stocks. It has been commercially propagated since 1943.

ROSENBERGER

A clone, Rosenberger was found in a grove of Lisbon and Villafranca trees in California. The fruit is somewhat like Lisbon and the tree is vigorous and prolific. It became popular in California in the 1960s.

ROUGH LEMON
(FLORIDA ROUGH, FRENCH, MAZOE or JAMBERI)
This is perhaps a hybrid of a lemon and citron, but has been classed as a lemon. A much travelled variety, it is believed to have originated in northern India, where it grows wild. It was carried sometime after 1498 by Portuguese explorers to south-eastern Africa, where it became naturalised along the Mazoe River. From there it was taken to Europe and then by Spaniards to the New World. Today it is naturalised in the West Indies and Florida. The peel is lemon to orange, rough and irregular, with large oil glands. The lemon-yellow pulp is medium-acid, with moderate lemon aroma and flavour.

YEN BEN
Similar to Lisbon, this variety is the main cultivar in New Zealand, supplying the Japanese export market. It is smooth-skinned with a thin rind and a low number of seeds. Over 60% of harvestable fruit develops in winter.

SWEET LEMONS (*C. LIMETTA RISSO*)
This is a general name for non-acid lemons or limettas, favoured in some parts of the Mediterranean. They are also grown in India, where they are called *mousambi*. The tree is large, resembling that of an orange. Common names for varieties of this species include sweet limetta, Mediterranean sweet lemon, sweet lemon and sweet lime. The fruits are usually insipid with a mild, sweet juice, said to taste like home-made lemonade without too much additional sugar. They are not usually grown commercially.

DORSHAPO
This is a sweet lemon that closely resembles Eureka in characteristics, except for its sweetness. It is named after plant explorers Dorsett, Shamel and Popenoe, who introduced it from Brazil in 1914. It is also grown to some extent in the Mediterranean but apparently not in the USA. It has very low acidity.

MILLSWEET
This, apparently, was introduced into California from Mexico and planted in a mission garden. It is grown in Italy.

OTHER LEMONS AND HYBRIDS
CITRUS VOLKAMERIANA
The volkamerian lemon is a hybrid of the *Citrus limon* (lemon) and the *Citrus aurantium* (sour orange). The fruits are rounded in shape and middle-sized. The skin looks like an orange peel and the pulp has a sour taste, close to that of the lemon. It is often used as planting for other species. It has a good resistance to frost.

CAMERON HIGHLANDS
This was discovered growing wild in the Cameron Highlands of Malaysia and taken to the USA. It is a small, round fruit with pale green flesh and many seeds.

ESCONDIDO
This fruit is found near the Escondido River in Nicaragua. It is an elliptical fruit with deep yellow, thick and oily peel.

VARIEGATED PINK LEMON
This variety has distinctive green and yellow variegated foliage. The lemons have pink flesh, clear juice and an acidic lemon flavour. New growth is pink-coloured. It is grown more for its foliage than for fruit quality or quantity.

MESERO
This lemon from Spain produces fruits appreciated for their quantity of juice and essential oils.

PERRINE
Perrine is a hybrid of lemon and lime. See the Limes section.

PONDEROSA (AMERICAN WONDER)
Ponderosa is not a true lemon. It originated during the 1880s. The trees are rather small and somewhat thorny and the large fruits are seedy, with yellow, thick, bumpy-textured peel. Ponderosa is more sensitive to cold than true lemons. It is grown as an ornamental.

ARMSTRONG
Discovered in California, in about 1909. It resembles Eureka but it usually bears near-seedless fruits.

AVON
This was first noticed as a budded tree in Florida.
A budded tree propagated from the original specimen
around 1934 produced heavy crops of fruits suitable for
frozen concentrate.

ALL ABOUT CITRONS (CITRUS MEDICA)

The citron was the first citrus fruit to be introduced to
Europe, by the armies of Alexander the Great, about 300
BC. It found a home in the Mediterranean region where it
has been cultivated ever since. Just to add to the
confusion, lemons are called *citrons* in France, although
there are considerable differences between lemons and
citrons, as I discovered when thinking I had bought a
bargain lot at a supermarket, only to find there was no
juice. I now know that *Cedra* are known elsewhere as
citrons.

The citron is not a typical citrus fruit. While the peel of
popular citrus species is discarded in favour of the inner
pulp and juice, the citron contains an extremely dry pulp
which has little taste or value. The bulk of the fruit
consists of the thick white rind, which grows strongly
against the inner pulp and is not easily removed. Some
varieties of citrons (etrog) are considered an important
part of the Jewish festival of Sukkoth. You can read about
this in a later chapter.

CITRON TREE
It grows as an open-headed shrub or small tree with
large, light green, lemon-scented leaves. The tree may
reach 2 to 4.5 m (8 to 15 feet). Foliage and fruit are
easily damaged by very intense heat and drought. Italian
producers keep the tree low and stake the branches. The
trees begin to bear fruit when three years old and reach
peak production after 15 years. They die after
approximately 25 years.

FLOWERS
The large flowers are fragrant and can reach 4 cm (1½ inches) across. They are coloured purple on the outside and grow in short clusters. Most have four to five petals, with 30 to 60 stamens.

FRUITS
These can weigh anything up to 4–5 kg (8–10 lb), if not picked early. They may vary in size, from 9 to 30 cm (3½ to 12 inches). The fruit may be ovoid, pear-shaped or some other form (see below). Various shapes sometimes occur on the same tree. When the fruit is fully ripe, the peel is very thick, very rough and yellow on the outside and white inside. The pulp is greenish, with little juice which is very acidic in most types. Fruits need to be picked, as they will not drop off naturally, causing branches to break off trees in winter. This damage encourages fungal growth.

COMMERCIAL CULTIVATION
The main producing areas, accounting for 90% of the citron market for food use, are around Italy (Sicily), Greece (Crete) and Corsica. Citron is also grown commercially in the mountainous coffee regions of Puerto Rico. Most is shipped in brine to the United States and Europe for processing. Citron is grown on several islands of the Caribbean and in Central and South America. It has been grown in Brazil for many years. Citron trees are not uncommon on some of the Pacific Islands but are rarely found in the Philippines. Etrog groves are found in Israel.

Citrons were originally grown in Europe to provide fragrant fruits. Later, the white pulp was served as a salad or with fish. This fruit is very tender and probably the least resistant to winter temperatures of all the citrus fruits. This is attributable to its tendency towards continuous growth. The best citron locations are those without extremes of temperature. The soils where the citron is grown vary considerably, but the tree requires good aeration.

Citron trees are often grown from cuttings taken from branches of two-to four-year-old trees which are quickly buried deeply in soil. The citron may also be budded onto rough lemon, grapefruit or orange stock, but the fruits do not grow as large as those produced from cuttings. The Etrog must not be budded or grafted if it is to be acceptable for use in religious ceremonies.

In Etrog orchards, Israeli growers are careful to protect the fruit, tying the fruiting branch securely in place. Fruit is protected from damage from twigs which might touch the fruit. To avoid having to move irrigation equipment through the groves, the trees are manually watered and frequently sprayed to eliminate destructive insects.
In India, a fruiting branch may be bent downwards so that immature fruit can be put into a shaped jar. The mature fruits, of the same shape as the jars, are sold as curiosities and are said to be intensely fragrant.

HARVESTING
The citron tree blooms nearly all year, but mostly in spring. These blooms produce the majority of the crop. The fruit takes about three months to turn yellow. To retain the green colour, firmness and uniformity needed for producing candied fruit, it must be picked when only 12 to 15 cm (5 to 6 inches) long and 7 to 10 cm (3 to 4 inches) in diameter. Mature trees yield an average of 30 kg (66 lb) per year but some trees have been known to produce as much as 68 to 100 kg (150 to 220 lb).

Etrog fruits are wrapped in hemp fibre immediately after picking.

PESTS AND DISEASES
The citron tree is subject to most of the pests that attack other citrus species. The citrus bud mite (*Eriophyes sheldoni*), citrus rust mite (*Phyllocoptruta oleivora*) and snow scale (*Unaspis citri*) are among its major enemies. Other problems lead to witches' broom, die-back and breaking of branches.

VARIETIES OF CITRON
Corsican and Etrog are the main varieties, but there is a whole range of others.

CORSICAN

The leading citron of Corsica and introduced into the USA around 1890. It is ellipsoid and furrowed at the base. A large fruit, it has a peel that is yellow, rough, lumpy, very thick and fleshy. The pulp is crisp, non-juicy and seedy. The tree is small and quite thorny, with some large spines.

ETROG (ETHROG)

The leading cultivar in Israel, the Etrog is ellipsoid, spindle-shaped or lemon-shaped. If not picked early, it will stay on the tree, continuing to enlarge for years until the branch cannot support it. For religious use, the fruit should be about 140 g (5 oz) and not oblong in form. The peel is yellow, rough, bumpy and faintly ribbed. The flesh is crisp, with little juice and an acid taste.

BUDDHA'S HAND/FINGERED CITRON

This fruit forms finger-like sections resembling a human hand. It is much liked in China and Japan for its delicate fragrance. The fruit has virtually no pulp, so is not eaten. It makes an unusual evergreen ornamental with multiple 'hands' hanging from the branches.

DIAMANTE (CEDRO LISCIO)

The leading cultivar in Italy and used by processors elsewhere. The long, oval fruit, furrowed at the base and broadly nippled at the apex, has yellow peel, smooth or faintly ribbed. The pulp is non-juicy and acidic.

YUZU (JAPANESE CITRON)

In autumn, this thorny tree produces lumpy, medium-sized, yellow to orange fruits. They are fragrant and highly prized as flavouring in Asian cuisine and for marmalade. The trees are amongst the hardiest of all citrus.

WHERE DO LIMES COME FROM?

TWO DIFFERENT TYPES OF LIME

Just so that nobody is confused, limes come from *Citrus aurantifolia*. This fruit has nothing to do with the tree known as common lime, basswood or linden in the UK, which is a deciduous tree of the *Tilia* family. We have two very large specimens of this beautiful tree in our garden in France. The French are very keen on making a sort of herbal tea from its flowers, which is called *tisane*. Yet another type of lime is calcium oxide, an alkaline chemical compound also known as caustic lime, burnt lime and quicklime.

TRUE LIMES

Some experts say that the only true lime is the *Citrus aurantifolia*, which was introduced in America by the Portuguese in the 16th century. Since then, it has been cultivated in Mexico and in Florida. Others suggest that the Tahiti lime (*Citrus latifolia*) is a different species. Some hybrids have been developed, such as the limequat, cross-breed of the *Citrus aurantifolia* and the *Fortunella margarita* (kumquat). So many varieties, so little space...

LIME (*CITRUS AURANTIFOLIA*)

TREE

This tree is a small evergreen, growing to about 3 to 5 m (10 to 16 feet). It is spiny and irregularly branched, with leaves that are pale green, oval and finely crenate. Some differences are apparent between the various varieties.

FLOWERS

The faintly fragrant, white flowers are small and are produced in clusters of between two and seven, which grow in different periods of the year. They grow in the axils, up to 5 cm (2 inches) across, and are either solitary or two to seven in a raceme, with four to six oblong, white spreading petals, tinged with purple when fresh.

FRUIT

The fruit, borne singly or in clusters of two to three at the twig tips, is round or slightly elliptical, sometimes with a slight nipple at the apex. The fruits are smaller than lemons at 2.5 to 5 cm (1 to 2 inches) diameter, much rounder and green or yellowish-green, except in some varieties that turn yellow when they are fully ripe. The lime pulp is greenish and sour, with about 10 sections. The peel is green, smoother and much thinner than that of the lemon and is rich in essential oils. The juice is acidic with a flavour that is quite distinct from lemons.

LOCATION FOR CULTIVATION
The lime comes from Malaysia and India and it is considered a natural hybrid of the *Citrus medica* (citron) with another species. Unlike other citrus trees, which are subtropical plants, the lime prefers a tropical climate, so is virtually unknown in the Mediterranean countries, except in Egypt. In the past the lime was exported from India to England to supply the crews of ships or sailors with vitamin C, to cure and prevent scurvy. Europeans took the lime to America in the 16th century and it became widely available throughout the West Indies.

Today limes are cultivated principally in Latin America and in the Caribbean, in Mexico and in South-East Asia. The lime has since become naturalised in Florida and is also grown in California. Some sweeter varieties are also grown. Limes are gathered when fully grown but still green, and shipped very soon after. Some limes will ripen to an orange colour if left on the tree, but they are always picked green. This possibly distinguishes them from lemons and other cross-bred citrus varieties.

In its most acidic form, a lime will have one and a half times as much acid as a lemon of the same weight. There are various kinds of limes, however, including sweet ones. The basic types of lime are Mexican and Tahitian limes.

MEXICAN LIMES
Mexican limes are small, with bright green skins and a very aromatic flavour. The Mexican lime tree is vigorous and may be shrubby or range up to 2 to 4 m (6 to 13

feet), with many slender, spreading branches. There are usually several, very sharp spines around 1 cm (⅜ inch) long. The peel is green and glossy when immature, pale yellow when ripe. The 6 to 15 segments are aromatic, very acidic and juicy. Key limes are closely related to the Mexican and have a pale yellowish-green fruit, very juicy with a strong, sharp flavour.

Mexican limes are more sensitive to cold than lemons. They thrive in a warm, moist climate with annual rainfall between 200 mm and 380 mm (80 to 150 inches). They do, however, tolerate drought better than any other citrus fruit. When there is excessive rainfall, the tree is subject to fungus diseases. These limes will grow on porous lava soil if there is enough rainfall, as well as sand and gravel. Limestone soils are also good.

The Mexican lime is usually propagated by seed because most seeds reproduce faithfully to the parent. In some areas, root sprouts from mature trees are taken up and transplanted into groves. Selected clones have been budded onto rough lemon or sour orange and these have proved to be more resistant to hurricanes, such as those hitting southern Florida: Hurricane Andrew in 1992 and Katrina in 2005. In Indonesia, this lime has always been air-layered.

On the Florida Keys, the trees produce some fruits more or less all the year round, barring hurricanes, but the two main seasons are May/June and November/December. The fruits are picked when the colour has changed from dark to light green, the surface is smooth and the fruit feels slightly soft to the touch. For processing, the fully ripe, yellow limes are gathered from the ground twice a week.

Withertip is a serious affliction of the Mexican lime in Florida. Wilt of seedlings in Florida greenhouses and twig die-back in India are some of the problems that have to be dealt with. When the weather is too humid, the Mexican lime is prone to attack by fungus, causing scab. It is also subject to algal disease, and oil spotting can be severe. In fact there seem to be a lot of nasties ready to attack limes, probably because of the tropical climate it likes.

VARIETIES OF MEXICAN LIMES
There are few varieties of the Mexican lime, as there is no great variation in the wild or under cultivation.

EVERGLADE
This has peel that is light yellow when ripe. The pulp is light greenish, has 8 to 10 segments and is aromatic, very juicy and of excellent quality and texture.

KAGZI
This variety is most commonly grown throughout India.

PALMETTO
The pulp is light greenish-yellow, of good quality and aroma and is very juicy.

YUNG (SPINELESS MEXICAN)
Said to be of unknown origin (though we might guess at Mexico, perhaps?), it was named after the man who introduced it into California, George Yung, around 1882.

TAHITIAN, BEARSS LIME OR PERSIAN LIME (*CITRUS LATIFOLIA*)
Some experts consider this a separate species, but according to others it belongs to the species *Citrus aurantifolia*. The *Citrus latifolia* is a variety of lime with oval fruit, slightly bigger than the Mexican lime fruit. These limes have a pale, finely grained pulp and a very acidic flavour. Some people say that there is a tang of pepper about them. They have been grown in California since 1875 and probably originated as a hybrid between the common lime and the citron. It is called Persian lime, even though it is unknown in Iran, and Tahiti lime because it reached the US via that country. The Tahiti lime comes in two varieties: Persian, which is oval and the size of an egg, and the Bearss, which is seedless and slightly larger. Both turn greenish-yellow when mature, but are best in flavour when they are green.

The Tahiti lime tree is moderately vigorous, growing up to 6 m (20 feet), with nearly thornless, widespread, drooping branches. The peel is vivid green until ripe when it becomes pale yellow. The pulp is light greenish-yellow when ripe, in 10 segments. It doesn't have the distinctive bouquet of the Mexican lime and is usually seedless. Tahiti lime flowers have no viable pollen.

It is presumed to be a hybrid of the Mexican lime and citron, although the exact origin is unknown. The Tahiti was probably introduced into the Mediterranean region by way of Iran, formerly called Persia. Portuguese traders probably carried it to Brazil, and it was apparently taken to Australia from Brazil around 1824. It reached California from Tahiti between 1850 and 1880 and had arrived in Florida by 1883, where it quickly took the place of the more sensitive small lime and the lemon. Following World War I, it became a well-established commercial crop. At first people viewed it as a green lemon. For some time, Canadians would not accept it because they were accustomed to the Mexican lime. Perhaps that's why the French call limes *'citron vert'* (literally 'green lemon').

The Tahiti lime is hardier than the Mexican lime. Even in southern Florida, drastic drops in temperature have made it necessary to protect lime groves with wind machines or overhead sprinkling. Like the Mexican lime, these trees tolerate limestone, deep sand or any well-drained soil. In land subject to standing water, lime trees are planted on raised beds.

This lime is usually propagated by budding onto the rough lemon, but in recent years many sweet orange and grapefruit trees have been used successfully. Today, 40% of the commercial Tahiti lime trees in the USA have been grown from air-layers.

Air-layered trees begin to bear fruit a year before budded trees but, as they mature, they generally do not yield as well.

Tahiti limes are harvested all year round, with the peak period in California between July and September. Tahiti limes do not require curing. The fresh fruits remain in good condition for six to eight weeks under refrigeration.

The citrus red mite may heavily infest Tahiti lime leaves and fruits. The tree is immune to withertip and moderately susceptible to scab and greasy spot. Red alga is a major problem, causing bark splitting and die-back of branches, leaving the tree subject to several viruses. The fruits are highly subject to oil spotting (oleocellosis).

VARIETIES OF TAHITI LIME
There have been few named cultivars of this type. Bearss, Idemor and Pond varieties are no longer grown in California for a variety of reasons, but were cultivated previously. Idemor is still grown in Morocco. Virus-free clones have taken over the Florida lime industry. That sounds a bit science fiction, don't you think?

SWEET LIMES
The sweet lime resembles the Tahiti lime in form, foliage and size of fruit. It is thought to be a hybrid between a Mexican-type lime and a sweet lemon or sweet citron. A native of India, northern Vietnam, Egypt and other countries around the coasts of the Mediterranean, particularly Italy, it is also found in tropical America. The sweet lime is interplanted with sweet orange or grapefruit trees to improve the yields. In India the trees are grown from cuttings. The sweet lime is also appreciated as an ornamental plant because it has a high cold resistance and its fruit lasts a long time on the plant. It is used principally as a rootstock.

Sweet limes are very hardy and similar to lemons, but less sour. They have a lower sugar content than some acid limes but are classified as sweet because of the lack of acidity. A Tahiti lime may have 6% citric acid content and oranges 1%, but the Indian sweet lime often has less than 0.1%. The peel, rich in essential oils, is yellow, and the pulp is green and juicy. This taste is popular in the Middle East and India, but not so popular in Europe or the Americas.

PURSHA (CITRUS LIME *PURSHA*)
It is probably a hybrid of a lime and an orange. The flowers, which blossom continuously from spring to autumn, are white and very fragrant. The fruits are rounded and the peel does not stick to the pulp, which is sweet, rather than sour and tasty.

PALESTINA (*CITRUS LIMETTOIDES*)
This is cultivated in India and Egypt. The peel is aromatic and smooth and has prominent oil glands. The fruit is very juicy, with practically no pips. Its taste is not greatly appreciated because the sourness doesn't exceed 0.1% and many consider it bland, or slightly bitter. Compared with other lime varieties it withstands cold and low temperatures better. It bears fruit late in the rainy season in India, when other citrus fruits are out of season.

OTHER INTERESTING LIMES
AUSTRALIAN LIMES
Although most limes are small, they can vary as they adapt to their natural habitat. The only two true citrus varieties from the Australian rainforests are both types of lime. The genus called *Microcitrus*, dating from 1915, with its very small, juvenile leaves and minute flowers, is found on the east coast. There is considerable variety and there are several unusual features. Here are a few examples.

AUSTRALIAN FINGER LIME *MICROCITRUS AUSTRALASICA*
It is found growing in subtropical rainforest as an under-storey tree with an average height of 6 m, on a range of soil types. The flowers occur singly in the leaf axils in spring and summer, and fruit is borne on the previous season's growth in autumn on seedling trees. Flowering and fruiting may occur several times a year, on grafted trees. Seedling trees have a long juvenile period of 5 to 17 years and few trees bear fruit annually.

The shape of the fruit is, as the name suggests, finger-shaped, but the species has a wide genetic diversity and fruit varies considerably in size, shape, colour, quantity of seed and degree of acidity. The mature skin colours of the finger lime range between crimson, blood red, purple, black, yellow and green. The pulp is green on maturity.

The finger limes can be used as a fresh fruit for garnish and for processing into a wide range of value-added products, such as salad dressings, beverages, sauces, marmalades, desserts, jellies and pastries. They contain up to 82 mg of vitamin C per 100 g. The finger lime has not yet been traded commercially in Australia, but is grown in California, where the fruit is sometimes called 'citrus caviar'. The main fruiting season in California is November to December.

That's something to watch out for, then: green finger limes, or red, purple-black or yellow finger-shaped limes. That in your G and T should get the party going!

ROUND LIME *MICROCITRUS AUSTRALIS*
This is the most vigorous of the Australian native citrus, growing to a height of 9 to 18 m. It is endemic to south-eastern Queensland. This species flowers in spring and bears rounded fruit which are 2.5 to 8 cm in diameter, with a rough greenish-yellow skin on maturity and pale green pulp. The fruit contains an acidic juice, similar to the finger lime, but does not have the variation in colour. The skin is very thick (up to 7 mm) and has potential for culinary use, such as grating into spice pastes, or for candied peel.

DESERT LIME *EREMOCITRUS GLAUCA*
Also known as the limebush, the desert lime is the only pronounced xerophyte in the subfamily, is extremely drought tolerant and able to withstand extremes of 45°C (113°F) and cold down to -24°C (-11°F).

The tree varies in size and shape, from a dense multi-stemmed thicket of 2 to 3 m in height, to a taller, more upright tree of 12 m. The fruit is roundish in shape and approximately 2 cm in diameter. The skin is a light yellow-green on maturity and contains large oil glands. The flower to fruiting time is the shortest of any citrus species, being 10 to 12 weeks. The species flowers mainly in spring and fruits ripen in summer.

VARIETIES THAT ARE NOT TRUE LIMES
RANGPUR LIME OR CANTON LEMON (*CITRUS LIMONIA*)
This tart, reddish-orange fruit is used like lime, although it is a sour mandarin from India. It is thought to have originated in South-East Asia and spread to China and India in cultivation so that by AD 1000 it was known in southern China. It makes a good ornamental tree, as the flowers and fruit overlap and provide added interest. It is popular in mixed drinks or sliced for ice tea. The juice is added to mandarin juice in India to improve the flavour. It is grown in India, California, Australia and Hawaii, and makes good marmalade.

EUSTIS LIMEQUAT
This is a cross between a Mexican lime and a kumquat. It is a prolific bearer of small, yellow, oblong fruit which can be used like limes.

PERRINE
This is a Mexican lime crossed with a Genoa lemon. It was created by Dr Walter Swingle and colleagues in 1909. It is lemon-shaped, with pale lemon-yellow, smooth peel and the pulp is pale greenish-yellow. The taste is very juicy, with a slight lime-like flavour and the acidity of a lemon.

KAFFIR LIME, KIEFFER
Also known as the Thai or wild lime, this is not considered to be a direct member of the lime species. This variety of lime has a very bumpy outer skin and is smaller in size. The grated peel and the leaves are commonly used as seasonings in Asian recipes for fish, meat, poultry, vegetables, marinades and chutneys. The flesh is not edible.

KUSAIE
This is more lime-like in aroma, although it is very similar to Rangpur. The tree is common in Hawaii and Trinidad, but little known elsewhere.

OTAHEITE LIME
This plant was introduced to Tahiti from France via England and, from there, to San Francisco. The fruit is round and almost 2 inches wide. The plant has fragrant

purple flowers and is sold as a potted plant near the end of the year in the USA, when it flowers and fruits at the same time. It is sometimes classified as a lemon.

GROWING ORNAMENTAL LEMONS IN BRITAIN

LEMONS FROM SEED?
Even in our less than hospitable climate, you can grow lemon or lime trees indoors if you have a conservatory or heated greenhouse. If the plants can make it through a British winter under cover, they can be put outside in tubs in the summer months. Just don't expect to get a continuous crop of fruit as you might in warmer parts of the world.

You can grow lemons or limes from undamaged pips from fruit, given time and patience, but any such tree will have to survive for about seven years before you see so much as a flower. Some specialist seed merchants supply seeds, although there doesn't seem to be a great choice around.

HARD GRAFT
Most citrus grown for indoor home use are dwarf varieties that are produced from cuttings grown or grafted on a dwarfing rootstock. This speeds up the process considerably and you won't get any nasty surprises at the size of the tree you are housing. By using cuttings or grafts from mature trees, you will grow a plant that is ready to begin fruiting much faster.

Recommended varieties for growing as ornamentals are *C. limon* Meyer, *C. l. Ponderosa* and *C.l.* Four Seasons, which is exactly that: a plant that flowers and fruits all year round. Fragrant white flowers will hopefully grow into small fruits, slightly sweeter than the average lemon.

LOOKING AFTER A LEMON TREE
With the right care and a little luck, your tree will bring you great enjoyment and last for years. Citrus trees need light, with at least four hours per day direct sunlight.

Normal room temperatures are fine, but in summer the plant will enjoy a patio in partial shade. Young trees are not hardy and will need to come inside as soon as there is a nip in the evening air. During active growth, plants need watering moderately, with the top of the compost drying out. Homes in winter have drier air, so if the plant is suffering, place a tray of pebbles under the pot. Lemons tend to grow slowly but potting on should be done in the spring, using a soil-based compost. Lemons need an average winter temperature of 7°C (45°F), although they fare better at around 10°C (50°F).

Lime trees need more heat than lemons, as they come from tropical regions. If you want to have a go at keeping one, try a miniature Tahiti or Persian lime. They are hardier than Mexican limes. Temperatures of 18 to 24°C (64 to 75°F) are needed for fruit to mature and these fruits may take up to 12 months to reach maturity. If they are grown in a greenhouse there must be good ventilation and shade from strong sunlight in summer.

MAIN PRODUCERS OF LEMONS AND LIMES

PRODUCTION
Mexico produces almost 12% of the global output of lemons and limes, followed by India, Argentina, Iran and Brazil, USA, Spain, China, Turkey and Italy. It is difficult to break down these figures into separate fruits because they seem to be reported together.

In terms of tonnage the main exporting countries are:
- Argentina
- Spain
- Mexico
- Turkey
- USA

EXPORT VALUE
In terms of export value, however, the list appears in a different order:
- Spain
- Mexico

- Argentina
- Turkey
- USA

LEMON ESSENTIAL OIL MAIN PRODUCERS ARE:
- Argentina
- Australia
- Brazil
- Greece
- Italy
- Peru
- Spain
- USA

LIME ESSENTIAL OIL MAIN PRODUCERS ARE:
- Brazil
- China
- Cuba
- Ghana
- Haiti
- Ivory Coast
- Jamaica
- Mexico
- Peru

The History Behind Lemons & Limes

LEMONS

Lemons are thought to have originated in South-East Asia, between India and southern China, where they have been cultivated for around 4,000 years. There is evidence of their existence in old oriental writings. Citrus is first mentioned in Chinese literature in 2200 BC. Some experts think that Burma and adjacent areas were the original home of the lemon. Others suggest that the lemon must have originated in the eastern Himalayan region of India, which is also the home of the citron. Archaeological evidence from the Indus Valley includes a lemon-shaped earring from 2500 BC. Natural hybrids with citron and lemon characteristics are abundant there. Lemons of the common Mediterranean type have not been found growing wild in any part of this region.

CHINESE LEMON JUICE

There is continuing disagreement as to the exact area of origin of lemons and how they spread to Europe. One theory suggests that the lemon is native to south-eastern China and was well known and cultivated before the Sung (or Song) dynasty (AD 960 to 1279), when bottles of lemon juice were allowed to be presented to the Emperor. This may suggest that the fruit was well known and widely grown long before that time. Another theory, however, holds that the lemon is not native to China, but was introduced into what is now Kwantung province, perhaps in the early part of the 12th century.

Another possible lead is that a Chinese writer in AD 300 spoke of a gift of '40 Chinese bushels of citrons from Ta-ch'in' in AD 284. Ta-ch'in is thought to be the Roman Empire. The citron was a staple, commercial food item in Rome in AD 301, so maybe this is true.

PERFECTLY PACKAGED

Lemons and citrons were the perfect commodity for traders, packaged in a durable skin which made them easy to transport by caravan or sea vessel. Citrus fruit travelled with other produce like figs to Turkey, Pakistan, Iran and routes further west. The citron was the first citrus to be carried to the Middle East, between 400 and

600 BC. Arab traders in Asia later introduced lemons to eastern Africa and the Middle East between AD 100 and 700. Much later the Crusaders distributed the fruit to other parts of Europe. The first uses for the lemon and citron in the Mediterranean were as ornamental plants in early Islamic gardens. Although the citron seems to have been known by the Jews before the time of Christ, the lemon does not seem to have been known in pre-Islamic times. A Jewish coin, dated 136 BC, bears a picture of the citron on one side.

EARLY ANTISEPTIC

Lemons were known in China, India and Mesopotamia for their antiseptic, anti-rheumatic and refreshing properties. Lemons were used as an antidote against poisons, as an astringent and to ward off evil.

GREEK TIMES

The ancient Greeks probably didn't know much about lemons or citrons very early on. Citrons were first used as decoration and to add perfume to linen. There is even a suggestion that they were used to protect clothing from moths. They were brought to the notice of the Greeks during the invasion of Alexander the Great into Media. The golden-yellow fruit attracted the attention of soldiers, who gave them the name of Median apples (*Mala medica*). Later on, soldiers discovered the fruit in Persia, so it became known as the Persian apple (*Mala persica*). There is a suggestion that the Median apple was thought by some to be identical to the fruit of the cedar (*Kedros*), from which the word citrus derives. This theory would perhaps account for the current French names, *citron* (lemon) and *cedre* (lime).

The first clear descriptions of the use of citrons for therapeutic purposes date back to the works of Theophrastus in the third century BC. He was a pupil of Aristotle and wrote books entitled *Enquiry Into Plants* and the six books of *Causes Of Plants*. The citron was the fruit described by Theophrastus. He described it as inedible, but capable of keeping away insects with its powerful fragrance.

The Greeks later used to plant lemon trees near olive trees to preserve them from parasitic attacks.

THE LABOURS OF HERACLES

The legend of the labours of Heracles (or Hercules, as he became known to the Romans) tells of the goddess Gaea producing some small, blooming trees with golden 'pommes'. These could have been oranges, lemons, citrons or the Median apples described above. The trees were given as a symbol of fertility and love, to celebrate the wedding between Hera and Zeus. They were kept in a garden guarded by the Hesperides, the daughters of Atlas, and by the dragon Ladon. Atlas held the world on his back, although some say he held up the sky.

Heracles, in his 11th labour, had the task of stealing the precious pommes. The myth tells that Heracles was advised to get Atlas to pick the apples. He offered to take Atlas's burden for an hour if he would pick the apples, which Atlas duly did. Atlas stole the pommes, but after having accomplished Heracles's task/labour of theft for him, he was called upon again by Heracles, who asked for his help, whilst he put a cushion in place to support the weight of the world. Atlas agreed, put the pommes on the ground and took the world, while Heracles took the pommes and ran.

ROMAN CITRONS AND LEMONS

It seems likely that the first citrus fruits known to the Romans were citrons. Mosaics found in a Roman villa at Carthage, in Tunisia, depict fruit-bearing citrus trees, and scientists have concluded that these citrons were the first citrus fruit known in Roman times. The citron is also mentioned by Pliny the Elder, a natural historian and philosopher, who lived from AD 23 to 79. He called the citron *malum medicum* due to its medical properties, showing that the original categorisation of apple was still followed. An apple a day, anybody?

Citrons or lemons have also been found in the ruins of Pompeii, destroyed by a volcanic eruption in AD 79 that also killed Pliny. The Orchard House was excavated in 1951, showing frescoes depicting various plants, including a lemon tree.

Pliny described the citron/lemon in his treatments and prescribed it as an antidote to various poisons. It seems likely, therefore, that the lemon was naturalised in Campania in the first century BC, even though it may have been a rare fruit.

The Roman scholar Athenaeus upheld the popular belief that lemon was a powerful antidote to poison. In his story, where two criminals are thrown to venomous snakes, the criminal who ate a lemon before being bitten survived, but the other met a violent death.

The Roman Emperor Nero (AD 37—68) was a regular consumer of this fruit, being obsessed with a premonition of poisoning. He was probably influenced by Dioscorides, a Greek physician who practised in Rome at the time of Nero. He had travelled widely and wrote one of the most influential herbal books of all times (*De Materia Medica*), and his ideas were still being used around 1600. He thought highly of the medicinal values of the bitter, wild-growing lemon.

In AD 150 the citron tree was said to be found growing around Naples and in Sardinia, although the fruit was still inedible. By about the 3rd century, cultivation had improved so that the fruit, a lemon, could be eaten, although it still seems to have been a rarity. Also in the 3rd century, the Romans believed that the lemon was an antidote to all poisons.

By the 4th century gardeners were growing lemons that bore fruit. Mosaics on a vaulted ceiling built for the Emperor Constantine (274—337) show citrons, lemons and oranges attached to branches covered with green leaves. It could be, however, that the artist had seen the lemons on his travels, or that they had been imported. Caelius Aurelianus recommended lemon juice for gout and fevers during the 5th century.

LOMBARDS AND DESTRUCTION

The Lombard invasion of northern Italy in 568 liberated most of Italy from the Byzantine or Roman Empire. However, most of the luxurious gardens of the rich were destroyed, probably along with the citron and lemon trees. Citron only survived in the south, in the Kingdom of Naples, in Sardinia and Sicily. By the year 1003, the citron was commonly cultivated at Salerno in south-west Italy and fruits called *poma cedrina* were presented as tokens of gratitude to the Norman lords, who had become the new masters. For centuries, this area supplied citron to Jews in Italy, France and Germany for their Feast of the Tabernacles.

MOVING ON

The next stage in the much travelled life of the lemon came around 1000, when the lemon was introduced by the Moors to Spain and North Africa. The Arabian geographer, Edrisi, writing in the 12th century, described the lemon as very sour and about the size of an apple. Although he wrote that it was a plant that only grew in India, he was wrong, as it had already been introduced to southern Europe. We probably get our word lemon from the Arab *limun* and the Indian *limu*.

THE NEW MILLENNIUM

The first written description of a lemon rather than a citron dates from an early Arabic text on farming from the 10th century, written by Qustus al-Rumi. The lemon became much more widespread after the Crusades (1095–1291), when it was found growing in Palestine. It reached Sicily before 1000, courtesy of Saracen invaders, and became more widespread in the Mediterranean region between 1000 and 1150, when the apricot, citron, sour orange, lemon and the shaddock had been introduced by the Arabs into Spain and northern Africa. The lemon was prized for its medicinal values in the palace of the Sultan of Egypt and Syria in the period 1174–1193. Crusaders spread the lemon further across Europe as they returned home or traded as conquerors. It then spread to parts of Asia. Another name for lemons, hasia, points to a possible culture of lemons in Iraq.

At the end of the 12th century, Ibn Jami, the personal physician to the Muslim leader Saladin, wrote the first treatise focusing on the lemon tree. After this time there was more frequent mention of lemons in the Mediterranean.

EGYPTIAN LEMONADE

Contrary to some sources, the citron and lemon were not known to the ancient Egyptians. There is some evidence that the lemon was grown in Egypt before 900. Egyptian peasants drank a date-and-honey wine, but by about the 14th century people along the Mediterranean coast were drinking *kashkab*, a drink made of fermented barley and mint, rue, black pepper and citron leaf. This was not quite lemonade, but the trade in lemon juice was well established by 1100. This is mentioned in the chronicles of a Persian poet and traveller called Nasir-i-Khusraw, who wrote the first reference to lemons in an account of life in Egypt under the Fatamid caliph al-Mustansir (1035—1094). A medieval Jewish community in Cairo from the 10th to the 13th centuries made bottles of lemon juice, (*qatarmizat*) with a lot of added sugar. This was both consumed locally and exported. Another reference is made — in one of the Arabian Nights stories — to Egyptian limes and Sultan oranges and citrons. These tales were collected in their present form in about 1450.

By the mid-15th century lemons were being cultivated on a wider scale in Italy and other parts of the Mediterranean. In 1494 lemons appeared in the Azores. Crusaders returning home via southern Europe probably brought the first citrus fruits to Britain. They didn't reach the Americas until this time either. Ships that arrived in the Mediterranean stocked up on lemons, paying for them with other valuable goods. The fruits bought were resold at very high prices in northern Europe, where the lemon was considered a product mainly used as an ornament or a medicine. It was only during the 18th century that lemons started to be used for culinary purposes.

CITRUS FRUITS AND THE AMERICAS

There were no native citrus fruits in the western hemisphere before the late 15th century. On his second voyage to the New World in 1493 Columbus took citrus seeds to Hispaniola, an island off Haiti, where he established the settlement of Isabella. Bartolome de las Casas, in his *Historia de las Indias*, which was written between 1520 and 1559, recounted that Columbus, with a fleet of 17 vessels, stopped in the Canary Islands to provide himself with supplies which included fruit and vegetable seeds. He visited the island of Gomera in the Canaries from 5 to 13 October, 1493. Lemons were amongst the seeds he collected. In about 1550 citrus trees including *limons* were found growing in abundance in the West Indies, including Haiti.

The citrus trees Columbus planted must have thrived, because about 30 years later there were too many of these trees to count.

At about the same time, lemons and other citrus fruits were introduced into Brazil by the Portuguese. In 1583 Fernando Cardim described planting in an orchard 'with many spine trees' which were taken to be lemon trees. By 1653 Peru was growing both large and small lemons.

LEMONS IN FLORIDA AND CALIFORNIA

Lemons were grown in California in the years 1751—68 and were being planted increasingly in north-eastern Florida in 1839. At this time Sicily was exporting to America. Commercial culture in Florida and California began soon after 1870 and grew to the point where 140,000 boxes of lemons were being shipped out of Florida alone. Then came a freeze in 1886, which damaged the trees, followed by diseases.

The unfavourable climate hampered the curing of the fruit and competition from California was strong. After a devastating freeze in 1894—95, commercial lemon cultivation was abandoned in Florida until 1953, when the interest in lemon-growing was revived due to the demand for frozen concentrate and for natural cold-press lemon oil. At the time, Florida was importing lemons from Italy for processing. Plantings grew to 8,700 acres by 1975, although bad weather again caused a 50% reduction by 1980. New varieties and plant breeding have made the industry more secure in recent years, although the weather cannot be accounted for.

CITRON PLANTING
Commercial citron cultivation and processing began in California in 1880. After inclement weather in 1913, the project was abandoned. From 1926 to 1936, there were scattered small plantings of citron in Florida. Again the weather affected the groves and today the citron is only grown in southern Florida for ornamental purposes or as a curiosity.

17TH-CENTURY LIPSTICK
Cesare Borgia, a Spanish prince from a rather famous family, sent presents of lemons and oranges to his wife while she was staying in France. Part of the reason was allegedly to impress Louis XII with his wealth.

The ladies of Louis XIV's court are said to have used lemons to redden their lips. I can think of less painful methods, especially in cold weather.

17TH-CENTURY HERBALS
Nicholas Culpeper was a physician and herbalist in the first half of the 17th century. He wrote two works entitled *A Complete Herbal* and *English Physician* and his advice on herbal remedies became popular for the next 250 years. His holistic approach, based on the four humours, used the principles of Greek/Arabic medicine and also used astrology for the prognosis of disease. He believed in remedies that were available to all people, so it is not surprising that they were considered important for so long. Some of his main work related to childbirth and gynaecology. I wonder what he would have made of some of the current research and claims about lemon juice (see the next chapter).

Culpeper refers to citrons, lemons and oranges in his works, but the only lime mentioned appears to be the Common lime or linden of the *Tilia* family.

Citrons and lemons were 'Cold in the first degree', whatever that meant. He also wrote: 'Moist in the first degree: The flesh of Citrons, Lemons, Oranges, viz. the inner rhind which is white, the outer rhind is hot.'

Culpeper recommended lemons for stomach ailments and to cool the breast. The heart could benefit from both lemons and citrons. One clue as to his studies of Greek medicine is that he said that citrons were to be used to 'resist poisons'. Lemons, along with all citrus fruits, must have been rare and expensive at the time he was practising.

RENAISSANCE GARDENS

Trees were grown in tubs and kept under cover in winter during the 17th century. Once glass-making techniques enabled sufficient expanses of clear glass to be made, places like the Orangerie at the Palace of the Louvre in Paris became regular features of Renaissance gardens. The Orangerie, built in 1617, inspired imitations elsewhere. An orangery became a must have feature for royal and aristocratic residences for the next 200 years, until greenhouses became more common after 1840.

SCURVY

Scurvy was described by Hippocrates (460–370 BC).

In the 13th century crusaders often suffered from scurvy and the disease has inflicted terrible losses on both besieged and besieger in times of war. Scurvy was a major limiting factor in marine travel, often being contributory factors in the deaths or disability of large numbers of the passengers and crew on long-distance voyages.
On these voyages there was a lack of fresh food; instead a diet of flour, preserved meat, often salted, and dry biscuits was 'enjoyed' by all travellers.

In 1536 the French explorer, Jacques Cartier, exploring the St Lawrence River, used the knowledge of local people to save his men from dying of scurvy. He boiled the needles of the Eastern White Cedar to make a brew that was later shown to contain 50 mg of vitamin C per

100 g. Nobody knew about vitamins back then, however, and the link with other foods seems not to have been made.

Gradually members of the medical profession and scientists came to the conclusion that the lack of fresh greens and acidic fruit was perhaps the cause, although other theories suggested that scurvy was due to a lack of hygiene. In 1614 John Woodall, the Surgeon General of the East India Company, published a handbook for apprentice surgeons aboard the company's ships. He described scurvy as resulting from a dietary deficiency. His recommendation for a cure was to give fresh food or, if that was not available, oranges, lemons, limes and tamarinds.

Obviously the advice from Woodall wasn't widely followed, because over 100 years later, in 1734, a Dutch physician called Johann Bachstrom published a book on scurvy, reiterating Woodall's recommendations. He said that '*scurvy is solely owing to a total abstinence from fresh vegetable food, and greens; which is alone the primary cause of the disease*'. It was not until 1747 that James Lind formally proved, through his experiments on seamen suffering from scurvy, that it could be treated and prevented, by supplementing the diet with citrus fruit such as lemons and limes. It eventually became law that ships had to carry enough lemon or lime juice for every man to have an ounce of the fruit daily, after 10 days at sea.

James Cook succeeded in circumnavigating the world (1768–71) without losing a single man to scurvy, probably because they picked up citrus fruit and fresh vegetables along the way. British sailors throughout the American Revolutionary period continued to suffer from the disease, however, particularly in the Channel Fleet. The eradication of scurvy was finally due to the chairman of the Navy's Sick and Hurt Board, Gilbert Blane. He finally put Bachstrom's and Lind's advice to use lemons and other citrus fruits into practice during the Napoleonic Wars, and other navies soon adopted this successful solution. Read on for more on this subject.

It was not until 1932 that the connection between vitamin C and scurvy was finally established.

During the First and Second World Wars, citrus mixtures and powders were given to soldiers and submarine crew. The Red Cross sent it to prisoners of war.

Lemons have also played their part in mountaineering achievements. Edmund Hillary and Tensing, the first men to reach the top of Mount Everest, apparently took lemon juice or powder with them. It isn't clear whether this was for dealing with high altitudes and lack of oxygen, or whether they used the lemons as a body energiser.

PECTIN
It had long been noted that some types of fruit needed additional fruit to obtain well-set jams and marmalades. This is because some fruits have little or only poor quality pectin. Pectin-rich fruits were therefore mixed into the recipe. In 1825 Braconnot discovered that pectin bonded with cellulose had a high commercial value.

In medicinal use, pectin increases viscosity and is used against constipation and diarrhoea as well as in wound healing preparations and medical adhesives. Pectin is also used in throat lozenges and cosmetic products.

During the commercial production of fruit preserves producers turned to apple juice and citrus peel, which was cooked to extract pectin. At first pectin was sold as a liquid extract, but nowadays dried powder is easier to store and handle than a liquid.

CITRIC ACID
In Europe, medieval scholars were aware of the acidic nature of lemon and lime juices. The 13th-century encyclopedia *Speculum Majus* (The Great Mirror), compiled by Vincent of Beauvais, shows such knowledge, but citric acid was first isolated in 1784 by the Swedish chemist Carl Wilhelm Scheele. He crystallised citric acid from lemon juice. It was not until 1860 that citric acid was produced on an industrial scale, based on the Italian citrus fruit industry.

LIMES

Limes are the smallest members of the true citrus family and native to South-East Asia or India. Documents do not distinguish them from other citrus fruits, so it is hard to be precise. An Indian medical work *c.* AD 100 refers to both the lemon and the lime as '*jambira*'. Later Arabic works use different words when referring to both. The first mention of the lime in literature seems to have been made by Abd-Allatif, in the 13th century. He wrote about 'balm lemon of smooth skin' being the size of a pigeon's egg.

The lime was also mentioned by Sir Thomas Herbert in 1677, when he referenced a site on Mohelia Island near the coast of Mozambique. He spoke of finding oranges, lemons and limes off Mozambique, during a voyage in 1626. He kept that quiet for a while, then.

Although limes are not mentioned specifically as one of the fruits Columbus collected in Gomera, they were flourishing on Hispaniola in the early 1500s. A naturalist called Oviedo, who lived in Santo Domingo from 1514 to 1525, wrote of limes as being well established there, as well as on the other islands. They were also found on the mainland, wherever Spaniards settled.

FLORIDA AND CALIFORNIA LIMES

In 1565 St Augustine established a community in what is now Florida. This is considered the date of the introduction of limes into Florida. It is possible, however, that explorers earlier in the century, around 1513, may have brought lime seeds to the continent. The indigenous people helped in the spread of limes through southern Florida. Two centuries later, wild groves of limes were found growing along the Indian River.

Limes were introduced into California by Franciscans, led by Fr Junipero Serra, when they were establishing missions. 'Foreign' plants including citrus were being cultivated in Baja (lower) California in the 18th century, so limes may have been amongst them.

19TH-CENTURY DEVELOPMENTS

While serving as US consul in Yucatan in 1838, Dr Henry Perrine shipped lime trees from Mexico to Indian Key. He had been granted a tract of land for the establishment of economic tropical plants. Sadly he met his death in an Indian massacre two years later whereupon the plantings were left to revert to the wilderness, but throughout the century the lime, known as Key, Mexican or West Indian lime, was growing in Florida. By the end of the 1880s there was some small commercial culture in Orange and Lake Counties.

LIMEYS

The British Navy gathered supplies of citrus fruit from the West Indies and other parts of the world like India to help prevent scurvy.

Limehouse is an area of Tower Hamlets, on the north bank of the Thames. It was originally part of London docks and takes its name from the warehouses where the fruit was stored after arriving by ship. Great warehouses preserved the limes for use by the British Navy. There were several seamen's hostels, pubs and churches in the area. The name 'Limey' seems to have come from the sailors of Limehouse. This became a pejorative term for all the British abroad.

Another suggestion is that the term derives from 'Lime juicers', because of the use of limes and lemons by the navy. It is more likely, in fact, that many of the limes were really lemons.

Nutrition And Health Benefits

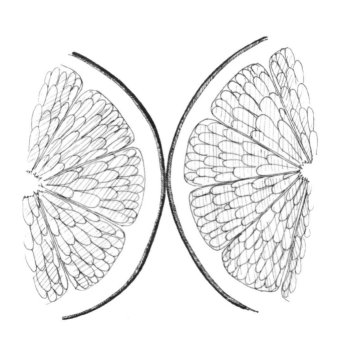

NUTRITIONAL INFORMATION

Practically everyone knows that citrus fruits are good for you, and that they are high in vitamin C, but there are a whole lot of other goodies stored away inside lemons and limes as well. Some of the nutrients are easily washed down in juice or by eating segments of the fruit, but the peels are also high in some vital nutrients. The problem is, how to get at them without destroying their goodness.

It is difficult to find agreement over the actual food values of lemons and limes because of the variability of different species. Broadly, lemons and limes contain the same elements, although there may be a variation in quantities and the percentage of the recommended daily intake. Lemons and limes aren't as easy to polish off in quantity as oranges, but you don't have to eat a lot of lemon for it to start doing you good. Given that 40% of the fruit is peel and only 58% is pulp, it makes sense to use some of the peel as well, but before you go mad, read the section on oxalates. Also, bear in mind that you may have waxed lemons, so they need to be washed very well before you use the peel, to get rid of chemicals. Unwaxed lemons are obviously not such a problem.

The following information has been collated from a variety of sources, because there seems to be a lack of consensus on given nutrients. This may be partly due to the quality of the fruit tested, or perhaps attributable to the fact that different species of fruit were tested. There is also a lot of variation, apparently, between ripe and under-ripe fruit, when it comes to vitamin C content. Stored fruit may also start to lose nutrients. I can't help wondering why sailors weren't given oranges instead of limes or lemons, as they contain a lot more vitamin C. Maybe it was easier to sell the sweet, juicy oranges for bigger profit. Poor sailors: stuck at sea all that time, feeling sickly, then they were told to suck on a lemon or lime! There is more vitamin C in lemons than limes, so eating limes must have been like drawing the short straw.

AVERAGE NUTRITIONAL VALUE OF LEMONS AND LIMES
These figures are for general interest only and should not be taken as categorically accurate in all cases.

	Lemon Pulp (per 100 g)	Lemon with Peel (per 100 g)	Lemon Pulp or Juice (per 100 g)
Carbohydrate	9 g	16 g	8 g
Protein	1 g	1.5 g	0.5 g
Fat	0.3 g	0.3 g	0.1 g
Water	89 g	82 g	91 g
Vitamin C	53 mg	129 mg	29 mg
Magnesium	4.6 mg	4 mg	8 mg
Calcium	26 mg	22 mg	19 mg
Phosphorus	16 mg	12 mg	15 mg
Iron	0.6 mg	0.8 mg	0.3 mg
Sodium	2 mg	6 mg	2 mg
Potassium	138 mg	160 mg	117 mg
Thiamine	0.04 mg	0.06 mg	0.03 mg
Riboflavin	0.02 mg	0.08 mg	0.02 mg
Pantothenic acid	0.19 mg	0.23 mg	0.21 mg

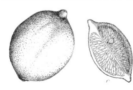

SOME OF THE NUTRIENTS AND BENEFICIAL COMPOUNDS IN LEMONS AND LIMES
CALCIUM
Both magnesium and calcium are needed for healthy bones. Calcium is essential for the normal growth and maintenance of bones and teeth. Requirements must be met throughout life, with long-term calcium deficiency leading to an increasing occurrence of osteoporosis. Women over 50 are particularly susceptible, when bones deteriorate and there is an increased risk of fractures.

CITRIC ACID (HYDROGEN CITRATE)
Citric acid is a weak acid found in a variety of fruits and vegetables, but is most concentrated in citrus fruits, particularly in lemons and limes, where it may comprise up to 8% of the fruit. It is a natural preservative and is also used to add an acidic or sour taste to foods and soft drinks. In biochemistry, it is important as an intermediate in the citric acid cycle and therefore occurs in the metabolism of almost all living things. It also serves as an environmentally benign cleaning agent (see the later section on cleaning). Citric acid is also produced chemically by dissolving tartaric acid in water and adding sulphuric acid and oil of lemon, but this type is of no therapeutic use. Citric acid is a known antioxidant and preservative.

FLAVONOIDS
Flavonoids are most commonly known for activity as antioxidants. They are sometimes referred to as bioflavonoids, because they are biological in origin. Interest in them has grown for their medicinal potential in preventing cancers and heart disease. They seem to work alongside vitamin C by modifying bodily reactions to viruses, allergens and cancer-producing agents, showing anti-microbial, anti-inflammatory and anti-cancer activity. Other foods high in flavonoids include onions, tea, red wine and broccoli.

Flavonoids on their own are of little direct antioxidant value and are not absorbed well by the body, but it is thought that they work by increasing uric acid levels. The body treats them as foreign compounds which it wants to get rid of as quickly as it can. At the same time it gets rid of other unwanted compounds and increases the antioxidant capacity of the blood. Hesperitin is the main flavonoid in citrus fruits.

In human nutrition it contributes to the integrity of the blood vessels. Hesperitin has anti-inflammatory effects and has been shown to reduce cholesterol and blood pressure in rats. Levels are higher in lemons than limes, although grapefruit has even higher levels.

Flavonols are a subclass of flavonoids. Flavonol glycosides have been proven to have antibiotic effects and may stop cell division in many cancer cells. In West Africa work has shown that lime juice has been a protective factor against contracting cholera.

IRON
Iron is found in every cell in the body. Iron links with protein to form haemoglobin, which is the oxygen transporter in your blood. Iron keeps your immune system healthy and helps to produce energy. Insufficient iron leads to anaemia.

LIMONOIDS
Limonoids are natural plant chemicals which are abundant in citrus fruit. They account for the scent of fresh lemon peel. Many plants used in traditional healing are rich in limonoids. They are currently being studied for a wide variety of therapeutic effects such as antiviral, antifungal and antibacterial qualities. They may also show effectiveness as insecticides.

MAGNESIUM
This helps to regulate the nerve and muscle tone. Magnesium keeps the muscles relaxed by preventing calcium entering the nerve cells. Insufficient magnesium may lead to muscle spasms or cramps, migraine, high blood pressure and fatigue.

PECTINS
Pectins are substances that are drawn from the pulp and peel of the fruit, but also from other fleshy fruit such as apples. Their industrial classification is E440. They are best known for helping jam to set (see later section). Pectins are soluble dietary fibres which have been used to treat cholesterol levels and as a prophylactic against poisoning. Pectins have many pharmaceutical uses, for example as a carrier of a variety of drugs for controlled release applications.

PHOSPHORUS
Phosphorus is a mineral that makes up 1% of the total body weight. It is present in every cell of the body, but

85% of the body's phosphorus is found in the bones and teeth. It plays an important role in the body's use of carbohydrates and fats, and in the synthesis of protein for the growth, maintenance and repair of cells and tissues. It is also crucial for the production of a molecule the body uses to store energy.

Phosphorus works with the B vitamins. It assists in the contraction of muscles, in kidney function, in maintaining the regularity of the heartbeat, and in nerve conduction. The main food sources are the protein food groups of meat and milk but there are small quantities in green vegetables. A meal plan that provides adequate amounts of calcium and protein also provides an adequate amount of phosphorus.

POTASSIUM

Potassium helps to contract all the muscles in the body. It is essential for heart function and maintaining normal blood pressure. Studies have shown that potassium reduces blood pressure and the risk of strokes.

THE VITAMIN B GROUP

VITAMIN B1 (THIAMIN)

Thiamin is one of a group of water-soluble vitamins that participate in many of the chemical reactions in the body. Thiamin helps the body cells convert carbohydrates into energy. It is also essential for the functioning of the heart, muscles and nervous system. A deficiency of thiamin can cause weakness, fatigue, psychosis and nerve damage. A high consumption of alcohol makes it hard for the body to absorb thiamin from foods. This can lead to a disease called beriberi.

VITAMIN B2 (RIBOFLAVIN)

Riboflavin has a number of important functions. It helps keep skin, eyes, the nervous system and mucous membranes healthy. It may help the body absorb iron from the food we eat and it helps produce steroids and red blood cells.

VITAMIN B3 (NIACIN)
Niacin helps the body turn the food we eat into energy. It also helps keep the nervous and digestive systems healthy.

VITAMIN B5 (PANTOTHENIC ACID)
Lemons and limes contain small amounts of this important vitamin; it is the key to the metabolism of carbohydrates, fats and proteins. In combination with zinc, it is claimed that B5 can prevent hair from turning grey in rats. It can promote resistance to the stress of cold immersion and may be tied to tumour inhibition. In combination with vitamin C it maintains capillary walls and promotes circulation. It is also said to be antibacterial and to promote pain relief.

VITAMIN C
Vitamin C is the main water-soluble antioxidant in the body and is vital for the healthy functioning of the immune system. It is good at preventing common colds and may also help to reduce recurrent ear infections. It is essential for healthy teeth and gums, helps wounds heal, helps fractures to mend and heals scar tissue. Deficiency has led to scurvy amongst sailors in the past.

Vitamin C helps Vitamin E become active and is associated with reducing inflammation caused by asthma and arthritis. It is also particularly effective in combating free-radical formation caused by pollution and cigarette smoke. Citrus fruits are particularly good sources of vitamin C, although lemons contain more than limes. One source suggests that the juice of one lemon supplies 35% of the daily requirement of vitamin C. Another suggests 55%.

POSSIBLE BENEFITS TO HEALTH
FROM EATING LEMONS AND LIMES

This section offers a brief survey of some of the research and possible beneficial effects to be gained by consuming lemons and limes. It should not be considered as an alternative to seeking professional medical advice for severe conditions, under any circumstances. Some of the remedies sound worse than the diseases, so I leave judgement up to you.

Firstly, here are a few precautions:
- Don't take concentrated lemon juice regularly. It should be diluted with water. Pure lemon juice contains acid which may harm the enamel of teeth.
- Lemon and lime peel is among a small number of foods that contain measurable amounts of oxalates. These occur naturally in plants, animals and human beings. When oxalates become too concentrated in body fluids, they can crystallise and may cause health problems, so anyone with an existing and untreated kidney or gallbladder problem may want to consider avoiding the peel.
- Some people develop dermatitis when handling limes for a long time. The practice of rolling the fruit between the hands before extracting the juice may coat the hands with oil. This in turn may be transferred to other areas, causing itching, redness and, sometimes, blisters.
- Fruits may be waxed to protect them from bruising during shipping. Plant, insect, animal or petroleum-based waxes are all used, although Carnauba palm is the most common source of wax. Other compounds, such as ethyl alcohol or ethanol, are added to the waxes for consistency. There may also be milk casein (a protein linked to milk allergy) or soaps for flowing agents. If you buy unwaxed lemons you know that these chemicals won't be present.

ACNE
Lemon juice is an astringent and kills many types of bacteria. Niacin, contained in lemons and limes, has been used successfully to treat acne. The best way to deal

with skin problems is to eat properly for a start.
A simple, topical remedy for acne is to apply lemon juice
regularly. This has shown beneficial effects in reducing
pimples and acne. Be aware that some sensitive skin
might not take kindly to acidic lemon juice, so try a small
area first.

Cut a slice of lemon and rub it gently over the affected
areas before going to bed. It will work all through the
night and you should wash it off thoroughly in the
morning.

Another method is to squeeze juice out of a lemon and
mix it with rose water. This mixture should then be
applied over the skin.

ANTIBACTERIAL PROPERTIES
Lemon juice is a powerful antibacterial. It has been
shown that the bacteria of malaria, cholera, diphtheria
and typhoid are destroyed in lemon juice. Drinking lemon
juice, either sweetened or salted, can apparently be an
effective preventive measure during epidemics of
cholera.

ANTI-CANCER PROPERTIES
Lemons and limes may contain properties that deter cell
growth in cancers. Flavonoids are known to aid the
immune system and may also prevent some cancerous
cell division.

An American research programme has suggested that
limonin, a long-acting limonoid found in citrus fruit, stays
in the system of some people much longer than the
phenols that tea and good quality dark chocolate provide.
Limonoids are thought to be powerful anti-carcinogens.

A few years ago researchers suggested that citrus pectin,
a natural chemical found in fruits, may help prevent
prostate and other cancers. It was claimed by research on
mice that clumping of cells forming tumours could be
prevented by modified citrus pectin. The cells would not
be able to attach to each other or to the walls of blood
vessels. However, research is at an early stage and

nobody is suggesting that this is a cure or secure treatment for cancer. Scientists are exploring the possibility of boosting pectin content in citrus fruits or using it to add health benefits. Lemons seem to have had the most effect so far. Pectins seem to be effective at delivering drugs to the colon effectively.

ANTI-INFLAMMATORY QUALITIES

Free radicals interact with the healthy cells of the body, damaging them and their membranes. This can cause a lot of inflammation in the body. Vitamin C has been shown to be helpful in reducing inflammation. It plays a role in fighting infection and may work to control inflammation which is linked to infection.

BLADDER PROBLEMS

Lemon juice is a diuretic as well as having antibiotic properties. It gives relief in kidney and bladder disorders.

BLEEDING

Pectins shorten the coagulation time of drawn blood, so were found to be useful in controlling haemorrhage or bleeding about 50 years ago. One suggestion was to drink lemon juice in very cold water to stop the bleeding. Another remedy suggests drinking the juice of three lemons a day in a glass of water to help with heavy periods.

CHOLESTEROL REDUCTION

Research suggests that citrus pectins can reduce cholesterol levels if consumed regularly. That doesn't mean we should stop taking medication. It means that eating fruit and vegetables as part of a balanced diet could perhaps put us at less risk. The average consumption should be about 5 g per day if we eat our five a day. A minimum of 6 g of pectin per day is described as particularly beneficial. That may have been suggested by a commercial producer, of course. Scientists are now investigating the potential cholesterol-lowering effects of limonoids.

COLDS AND FEVER

The vitamin C in lemon juice, along with its antibacterial effects, is said to restrain influenza, malaria and cold bugs. I always resort to a soothing drink of honey and lemon when I have a bad cold. Use a teaspoonful of honey with about two tablespoons of fresh lemon juice in a cup of boiled water. You can add more honey if you wish. See below for sore throats as well. Alternatively, lemon juice with salt or ginger can be taken to relieve a cold.

Lemon juice gives good relief in cases of high temperature or fever. About one to two tablespoons of lemon juice in water make an effective thirst-quenching drink in relieving patients suffering fevers with extreme thirst and a very hot, dry skin.

Boiled slices of lemon, root ginger, cinnamon and honey make a punchy remedy for colds and flu, if you have the energy to make it, that is.

ZEST FOR NO LIFE?

Throughout history, women have used objects such as sea sponges or wool as a sperm barrier in combination with lemon juice. There are even reports of half-lemons being inserted into the vagina 300 to 400 years ago. Ouch!

Lemon and lime juice has been tested as an anti-viral contraceptive that can easily be obtained in the developing world. Women researchers in Australia have said that using the juice caused no pain. Acids such as lemon juice can inactivate sperm and kill some viruses but, although lemon juice was used historically as a contraceptive, it is not known how much damage this did directly to the vagina, cervix or uterus. Considering that vinegar was used in Victorian times as a cheap, if not reliable, contraceptive, this information shouldn't come as a great surprise. It's best to rely on more modern methods, I think.

In Papua, islanders who were worried that homosexual males might become pregnant held ceremonies during which they fed them limes to avoid conception. Well, no problem there, then — a safe method at last!

DETOX
Ancient Indian medicine says that a cup of hot water with lemon juice in it tones and purifies the liver.

Another suggestion is to take lemon juice mixed with cold water and honey on an empty stomach early in the morning. Warm water may be used occasionally to get relief from constipation.

DIGESTIVE DISORDERS
Lemon juice is said to aid the bowels in eliminating waste more efficiently. The digestive qualities of lemon juice also relieve indigestion symptoms such as heartburn, bloating and belching. In human digestion, pectin passes through the small intestine more or less intact. In the large intestine and colon, micro-organisms break down pectin and liberate fatty acids that have a positive influence on health. Pectins reduce the rate of digestion by immobilising food components in the intestine. This results in less absorption of food. Due to a large water-binding capacity pectins give a full-up feeling, thus reducing food consumption. These attributes are used in the treatment of disorders related to overeating. Pectins have also been used to treat diarrhoea, especially in children. The antibacterial qualities of lemons also help with a range of diseases causing diarrhoea.

For the relief of heartburn, add a teaspoon of fresh lemon juice to half a glass of water. Lemon juice in hot water has been advocated as a daily laxative.

For stomach upsets or hangover sickness, try drinking the juice of a lemon mixed with half a teaspoon of bicarbonate of soda in two or three tablespoons of water.

FOOT CARE
This sounds quite soothing. For sore or tired feet, soak them in hot water and then rub half a lemon over the feet, including the soles and heels. Pat them dry.

This is less practicable: tie a slice of lemon over a corn or callous before going to bed. I suppose you could use an old stocking or foot of some tights to keep it in place.

GOUT
Taking lemon juice prevents the deposit of uric acid in the tissues and reduces the possibility of an attack of gout.

HALLITOSIS
Lemon is used as a local antiseptic for offensive breath and also as an internal alkaliser. A drink of lemon juice sweetened with a little honey, two to three times daily, may guarantee sweet breath. It depends whether you've been on the garlic or something worse, I suppose!

HANGOVER HEADACHE
A suggested cure for a headache caused by over-indulgence of the grain or grape is to take lemon juice with a few teaspoons of hot tea. You might not need that packet of pills.

HEART AND CIRCULATION
Since free radicals can damage blood vessels and can make cholesterol more likely to build up in artery walls, the many health benefits available from vitamin C can be helpful in preventing the development and progression of atherosclerosis and heart disease. The pantothenic acid (vitamin B5) in lemon is said to strengthen blood vessels and prevent internal haemorrhage. The high potassium level is also beneficial to the heart. There's a good reason for eating your 'five a day' fruit and vegetables.

HEPATITIS
Vitamin C is important in strengthening the immune system. Citrus juice also encourages bile secretion and is valuable in the treatment of jaundice. Having had the misfortune to contract Hepatitis A as a teenager (luckily, not the worst form of hepatitis) I was advised to eat a dairy free, low fat diet and to eat at least two oranges a day for several weeks.

HICCOUGHS
A drink of lemon juice is said to be the best cure for severe, obstinate hiccoughs, although I seem to remember that vinegar also claims this distinction.

HIV TREATMENT?

Lemons have been used to control the spread of the HIV virus, and it has even been claimed in research studies that they can kill the HIV virus. Keeping a healthy liver is a critical step in the health and recovery of both cancer patients and those with HIV and AIDS. One claim is that combining whole lemon (including pith, peel and seeds) with extra virgin olive oil produces amazing results. The ingredients are blended with spring water and drunk on a daily basis. The lemon and olive oil, when taken together, act as a potent liver and gallbladder flush and detoxify the liver. The research claims that restoring the pH of your saliva helps you to absorb the nutrients from the food you eat. Drinking puréed lemons with olive oil every day sounds like hard work and not a substitute for conventional medicine.

INTESTINAL WORMS

Lemon and lime juice has been used in destroying intestinal worms. Yuck. Don't ask which sort. In Malaya lime juice is used with oil to expel the disgusting parasites.

OSTEOARTHRITIS AND RHEUMATOID ARTHRITIS

Some people think that avoiding acidic fruit such as oranges, lemons and grapefruit helps arthritis. Others believe that vegetables from the nightshade family, including potatoes, tomatoes and peppers, should be avoided. There is no evidence that either of these food groups makes arthritis worse. The antioxidants are more likely to be doing good to the whole body. Research has shown that people who eat plenty of fresh fruit and vegetables, particularly those containing vitamin C, have a lower risk of developing inflammatory arthritis. This doesn't suggest that going over the top with vitamin C is the answer. Like with all diets, the point is that a balance of foods, including a variety of fruit and vegetables, will promote the best health outcomes.

Studies over the past few years suggest that long-term use of vitamin C, i.e. with high doses or vitamin supplements, may worsen the severity of osteoarthritis of the knee, but normal daily amounts (75 mg for women and 90 mg for men) are not going to cause a problem.

Another study suggests that protection from rheumatoid arthritis can be gained by eating vitamin C-rich foods, such as lemons and limes. Over 20,000 people who were free from rheumatoid arthritis kept food diaries over a period of time. People who consumed the lowest amounts of vitamin C-rich foods were more than three times more likely to develop arthritis than those who consumed the highest amounts.

Over an eight-year period researchers in the UK compared around 70 participants who developed arthritis with twice that number who remained free of arthritis. The first group were found to have consumed less fruit and vegetables than the second. Researchers found that participants who ate the least fruit and vegetables had twice the risk of developing inflammatory arthritis.

One suggested dose for easing rheumatism is 30 ml (2 tablespoons) of lemon juice diluted in water, taken three times a day, an hour before main meals and at bedtime.

As a massage, lemon juice and olive oil can be gently rubbed into the joints after a patient has had a hot bath.

POISONING
Maybe the Greeks and Romans were right after all to recommend consuming lemons to treat poisoning. They have been shown to be effective in removing lead and mercury from the gastrointestinal tract and respiratory organs. Vitamin C also contributes, by preventing nasty free radicals causing problems from pollution and smoking. Lemon juice is supposedly given to counteract narcotic poisons, especially opium. In the past, citron juice with wine was considered an effective purgative to rid the system of poison. In parts of Central America, ground up lemons are combined with other ingredients and given as an antidote for poison.

RINGWORM
Although not a common occurrence, I did see one or two cases in children during my teaching career. In some countries ringworm is widespread. It is a painful and

irritating, infectious skin condition. The suggested home treatment is to use half a lemon or lime, sprinkled with salt. This is applied to the affected area by rubbing slowly and then with more force. Wash the area in warm water and dry thoroughly. Better still, see a doctor.

SCURVY

Scurvy is caused by vitamin C deficiency, and can be prevented by having 10 mg of vitamin C a day. An early sign of scurvy is fatigue. If deficiency is untreated, later symptoms include bleeding and bruising easily. A suggested treatment is 30 to 60 ml (2 to 4 tablespoons) lemon juice diluted in water, given every four hours. The source doesn't say for how long this needs to go on, however. Another suggested remedy is to drink a mixture of one part lemon or lime juice, three parts of water and a quantity of sugar or honey.

In the Middle Ages, the citron was given as a remedy for seasickness.

SORE THROAT

For a sore throat, gargling with fresh lemon juice diluted with water is recommended. Dilute the juice of half a lemon with half as much water. See advice for colds as well. The honey and lemon drink is great.

SPLINTERS

To remove a splinter, cut a slice of lemon and place over the splinter. Cover with a bandage and leave overnight for the lemon to draw out the splinter and any infection that has accumulated.

STINGS, BITES AND ABRASIONS

Lemon juice is also said to relieve the pain of bee stings. It acts as an antihistamine. The juice is also good for treating cuts and scratches, if you can stand the stinging. A few drops of lemon juice serve as a disinfectant. Combined with papaya juice it is said to be extremely effective in cases of athlete's foot. Lime juice is also said to relieve mosquito bites. I've tried using lemon juice, which isn't very effective.

STRESS
A Japanese study into the effects of aromatherapy found that lemon essential oil in vapour form reduced stress in mice. Well, what can I add? Only that it is said to act as a sedative for the nerves.

SUNBURN
I've seen a few references to lemon juice being used as a lotion in sunburn. I assume that this is diluted in cold water first.

SUPPLE FEET
I've recently heard of a dancing teacher recommending keeping feet and joints pliant with olive oil and lemon juice massage before and after lessons. That may be good for walkers as well.

TOOTH WHITENER
Use the rind of a lemon to rub on your teeth and gums to whiten them. Always rinse off with water immediately.

OTHER CLAIMS TO FAME
- In Italy, the sweetened juice is given to relieve gingivitis and inflammation of the tongue.

- In West Africa lemon juice is used to treat gonorrhoea. An infusion of the bark or peel of the fruit is given to relieve colic. Citrons are used to relieve rheumatism.

- In India, the peel is a remedy for dysentery and is eaten to prevent halitosis.

- In China, candied peel is used to tone the stomach and increase the appetite as well as a stimulant, expectorant and tonic.

- In Malaya, a drink of lemon juice is taken to drive off evil spirits. Lime juice is taken as a tonic and to relieve stomach ailments. The pickled fruit, with other additions, is used as a poultice on the head.

- In India, pickled lime is eaten to relieve indigestion. The juice of the Mexican lime is regarded as an antiseptic tonic for a whole range of ailments. Lime leaves are poulticed onto skin diseases and onto the abdomen of a new mother after childbirth. The stewed leaves are also used as eye drops and to bathe a feverish patient. They are also used as a mouthwash and gargle in cases of sore throat and thrush.

- Lemons and limes have been used after childbirth to control bleeding and as an antispasmodic.

- In Spain, a syrup made from citrus peel is used to flavour nasty tasting medical preparations.

- In some tropical lime-growing countries undiluted lime juice is used to kill bacteria and stop diarrhoea. Ginger and lime are given for treating nausea.

- In some parts of the world, lemon juice is used as a substitute for quinine in malarial conditions and for reducing the temperature in typhoid.

- Dabbing warts with lemon juice may help to get rid of them, if applied regularly for several days.

- Some people say that lemons are effective in counteracting depression and confusion, and increase concentration . . . Now, could somebody remind me, what was I saying . . . ?

Industrial Uses

INDUSTRIAL USES OF LEMONS AND LIMES

As well as the obvious culinary uses of lemons and limes there are a number of other applications. Many of these relate to citric acid.

CITRIC ACID

Citric acid is such useful stuff that it is used in many industries, for example:

- as a food preservative
- in pharmaceuticals
- in household cleaners
- as a water softener
- in explosives
- in photography

Citric acid is used as a flavouring and preservative in food and beverages, especially soft drinks. It is known as food additive E330. Citric acid was first isolated in 1784 by a Swedish chemist called Carl Wilhelm Scheele, although people back in the 8th century seem to have been aware of some of the properties of lemon and lime juice. Scheele crystallised it from lemon juice. It wasn't until 1860 that citric acid was produced on an industrial scale, when it was based on the Italian citrus fruit industry. In 1893 Wehmer discovered that citric acid could be manufactured, but there was no real need until World War I, when exports from Italy were disrupted. Nowadays, commercially produced citric acid is a major component in a whole range of industries.

In 1953 a biochemist, Sir Hans Adolf Krebs, received the Nobel Prize for Physiology. He defined a series of chemical reactions of central importance in all living cells that use oxygen as part of respiration, which became known as the Krebs cycle, tricarboxylic acid cycle or the citric acid cycle. This cycle is central to the metabolism of nearly all living things and the source of 65% of the food-derived energy in higher organisms, when carbohydrates, fats and proteins are converted into usable energy.

As an aside, the unfortunately named Krebs inadvertently gave rise to the idea that citric acid would cause cancer because *Krebs* is also the German word for cancer.

WHAT IS CITRIC ACID?

Citric acid is the most widely used substance for making products sour or mildly acidic. It is used as a pH-control agent. Its salt, sodium citrate, is another frequently used additive. About 8% of a lemon or lime is citric acid. Citrate is a salt or ester of citric acid. Citrate is more commonly used than straight citric acid.

At room temperature, citric acid is a white crystalline powder. It can exist either as a powder or as a liquid, with water. When heated above 175°C (347°F), it decomposes through the loss of carbon dioxide and water.

PRECAUTIONS

Contact with dry citric acid or with concentrated solutions can result in skin and eye irritation. Protective measures should be taken when handling these materials. A small number of people are sensitive to or intolerant of citric acid, so being aware of the number of uses must be a nightmare.

USES OF CITRIC ACID IN THE FOOD INDUSTRY

Citric acid is used as a natural food preservative and is also used to add an acidic or sour taste to foods and soft drinks. It is recognised as safe for use in food by all major national and international food regulatory agencies. Any excess acid is easily eliminated from the body. Its main uses are:

- a sharp-tasting flavouring;
- a preservative;
- an improver of stability and quality. It combines with naturally occurring trace metals in foods to prevent discolouration;
- in wine production, where it combines with iron to prevent the formation of tannins which cause cloudiness;
- in brewing, where it reduces excess losses of sugars from the germinated barley;
- creation of an acidic environment to discourage the

growth of certain bacteria, yeasts and moulds;
- in cheese making, where it speeds up the production of the necessary acidic environment for enzyme activity. Traditional souring by lactic acid, caused by bacteria, takes longer. Citric acid is also said to improve the texture of processed cheese;
- in confectionery, where it controls sugar inversion and improves gel setting and helps artificial sweeteners taste better;
- helping powdered milk or cream to mix properly when added to hot drinks;
- in the production of rape seed oil, to prevent rancidity.

Citric acid can be found in a wide range of products, including:

- non-alcoholic drinks, especially carbonated ones
- bakery products, biscuits and cake mixes
- beer, cider and wine
- cheese and processed cheese spreads
- frozen fish
- ice creams and sorbets
- jams, jellies, preserves, syrups and sweets
- frozen croquette potatoes and potato waffles
- packet soups, tinned fruits, sauces and vegetables
- dairy and non-dairy creamers for coffee

MEDICINAL AND PHARMACEUTICAL USES
Citric acid is used in the biotechnology and pharmaceutical industries. It is used to make a material passive in relation to another material before using the materials together. It is used because it is non-hazardous to dispose of, unlike compounds such as nitric acid. Other uses:
- Citric acid is used to enhance the effectiveness and performance of other antioxidants.
- Citrate salts are used to deliver minerals in many dietary supplements.
- The buffering properties of citrates are used to control pH in pharmaceuticals.
- In the form of calcium citrate, it is used as a dietary calcium supplement. Studies have shown that calcium

citrate is more bio-available than calcium carbonate.
- It is used with bicarbonate of soda to create effervescence for ingestion in powders and tablets.
- Citric acid is commonly used as a buffer to increase the solubility of brown heroin. Citric acid sachets have been used as an inducement to get heroin users to exchange their dirty needles for clean needles in some countries. Other acidifiers used for brown heroin are ascorbic acid (Vitamin C), acetic acid and lactic acid. A drug user will apparently often substitute lemon juice or vinegar.

SOAPS AND CLEANING

The ability of citric acid to bind to metals makes it useful in soaps, shampoos and laundry detergents. The largest industrial application for citrates is in detergents.
In liquid detergents, sodium citrate increases the effectiveness of the wetting agents. It is highly soluble and biodegradable. It lets cleaners produce foam and work better in hard water areas, without the need for water softening.
- It regenerates the ion exchange materials used in water softeners by stripping off accumulated metal ions.
- It is the active ingredient in some bathroom and kitchen cleaning solutions.
- As a hard surface floor cleaner it acts as a scale dissolver and prevents re-deposition.
- It is used along with sodium bicarbonate in a wide range of effervescent products, such as bath salts, bath bombs and cleaning of grease.
- On hair it opens the cuticle or outer layer and can be used to wash out wax and colouring from the hair.
- Citric acid is also added to hair care formulations to adjust the pH. It can also be used as a buffer and prevent discoloration.

OTHER INDUSTRIAL APPLICATIONS OF CITRIC ACID
- Citric acid is one of the chemicals required for making an explosive similar to acetone peroxide. Large quantities of citric acid would be required, so the purchase of it for illegal or terrorist activity would be a bit of a give-away.

- Citric acid is used as a stop bath in the developing process of film photography. The developer is normally alkaline, so a mild acid will neutralise it and increase the effectiveness of the stop bath, compared with plain water.
- Citric acid is used in nuclear reactors to remove mill scale from welding operations.
- In oil well acidising it helps to prevent the formation of insoluble gels of iron hydroxide. These gels interfere with pumping operations.
- Sodium citrate is used in radiator cleaning formulations.
- Citric acid is used in cleaning bilges of rust and in desalination units aboard ships.
- In the paint industry citric acid is used to retard the setting of titanium dioxide, the most common pigment used in paints.
- It is added to pulp slurry prior to bleaching during paper-making.
- In pet food and animal feed it is used as a flavour enhancer and also to increase the efficiency and uptake of feed.
- In plating it controls the deposition rate of metals in both electroplating and non-electro operations.
- In textile finishing, citric acid is used to adjust pH, as a buffer and as a binding agent in dye operations and durable-press finishes.
- It is used to bind copper in formulations used to kill algae in reservoirs and natural water.
- Abattoirs use it to prevent the coagulation or clotting of fresh blood.
- Citric acid and other components are added to balance the flavours of air-cured tobacco. It is also used in cigarette paper to control the burn rate, ensuring that the tobacco and paper burn at the same rate.
- Citric acid can be used as an environmentally friendly way to clean circuit boards prior to soldering.
- Citric acid is added to concrete formulations to slow down the setting rate and reduce the amount of water required.

OTHER USES OF LEMONS AND LIMES IN THE FOOD INDUSTRY

PECTIN
Pectin is a white or light brown powder, derived from the cell walls of some plants, especially citrus varieties. Lemon and lime pulp and peel are good sources. Pectin is classified as food additive E440.

Braconnot first discovered pectin in 1825. One of the main raw materials for pectin production is dried citrus peel, a by-product of juice production. The pectin is extracted by adding hot dilute acid at pH values from 1.5 to 3.5. In the 1920s and 1930s, factories were built that commercially extracted pectin from citrus peel. Approximately 40,000 metric tons of pectin are produced every year, worldwide.

THE PROCESS
At first pectin was sold as a liquid extract, but nowadays it is often used as dried powder which is easier to store and handle. The process takes some hours to extract the pectin and it goes into a solution. After filtering, the extract is concentrated in vacuum and the pectin is then precipitated by adding ethanol or isopropanol. It is then separated, washed and dried. After drying and milling pectin is exchanged with sugar, calcium salts or organic acids to create specific conditions in a particular application. Different kinds of pectins can therefore be obtained. In an acid solution, usually citric acid and in the presence of sucrose, the pectins form gelatines.

USES OF PECTIN
FOOD
Pectin is mainly used in food as a gelling agent in jams and jellies, but also in fillings, sweets, as a stabiliser in fruit juices and milk drinks and as a source of dietary fibre. It is also used for thickening and emulsifying. For household use, pectin is sometimes sold as an ingredient in preserving sugar or sold as 'sugar with pectin', where it is diluted to the right concentration with sugar and some citric acid to adjust pH.

Pectin can also be used to stabilise acidic protein drinks, such as drinking yoghurt, and as a fat replacement. Typical levels of pectin used as a food additive are between 0.5 to 1.0%, which is about the same amount of pectin as there is in fresh fruit.

MEDICINAL
In the pharmaceutical industry quick-setting pectins are used in anti-diarhhoea applications as well as against constipation — input and output, then? That sounds a little worrying to a novice like me.

Pectin is also used in throat lozenges because it forms a soothing layer over mucous membranes. In cosmetic products, pectin acts as stabiliser. Pectin is also used in wound healing preparations and medical adhesives, such as colostomy devices.

ANIMAL FEED
In cattle fodder, pectin is used to improve the animals' digestion and energy concentrations of the feed.

CANDIED PEEL
This is produced from the peel of lemons and limes after juice or oil extraction, but most peel is made from citrons. Most of the citrons grown today are used for making candied peel for baking and confectionery use, where they make their way into fruit cakes, Christmas puddings, buns, sweet rolls and sweets.

METHODS OF PREPARATION
Candied peel can be prepared by boiling the peel in syrup and then exposing it to the air until the sugar is crystallised. First of all the fruits are halved, and the pulp is removed. In some countries the fruit is then immersed in salt water to ferment for about 40 days. The brine is changed every couple of weeks, before returning it to denser brine in wooden barrels for storage and for export. To make the candied peel the fruit has to be partially desalted and boiled to soften the peel. It is then candied in a strong sucrose or glucose solution before drying or putting into jars.

Another method is to desalt the peel, dry at 42°C (108°F) and pack in polythene. This reduces the weight by 95% and lowers shipping costs. A further method blanches cubes of citron for 30 seconds at 76°C (170°F). This can then be candied immediately, saving storage and shipping costs.

Much of this candying work is carried out in Britain, France and the USA.

QUALITIES OF PEEL
Different qualities are produced: glacé peels are covered with a thin coating of glacé sugar, while candied peels are covered with a heavier coating which is allowed to dry with a sediment of sugar in the cup.

LEMON AND LIME JUICE
LEMON JUICE
Lemon juice is largely imported as a source of citric acid, but is often mixed with lime and bergamot juice. It does not keep well, and several methods have been tried for preserving it. Juice should be pressed fresh for pharmaceutical purposes. In Europe, most juice is extracted in December and January. Argentina is the main world producer of concentrated lemon juice, followed by the USA. Seventy per cent of Argentine lemons are used for juicing.

There are different types of concentrated lemon juice, with different degrees of acidity. Approximately 17 kg of lemons are needed to obtain 1 kg of concentrated juice. This may vary according to weather conditions.

Clear lemon juice used to be very difficult and time-consuming to produce. In traditional methods the clarification process involved allowing the juice to stand for several weeks, during which time the juice had to be protected against oxidation and also against undesirable microbiological activity. Nowadays the process takes only six to eight hours, using clarifying centrifuges and enzyme action. Whereas separators were used for removing tissue particles of the fruit out of the press juice, or fining agents during the clarification process, decanters have replaced the presses in many commercial enterprises.

LIME JUICE

Fresh limes are perishable and it is often difficult to get them to the fruit market in a state where they still fetch a good price. Making the limes into lime juice can avoid many of these problems. The technology required is simple and due to the very acidic juice of limes (a pH of 2.0), spoilage problems are minimised. Lime juice is popular as an important ingredient in cooking, or can be made into a drink. The skin can be incorporated into lime pickle to reduce wastage. The yield of juice from whole limes is expected to be around 40%.

Lime juice is very acidic and workers are provided with protective gloves to avoid damage to the hands. Only inert materials can be used to process lime juice, which will rapidly corrode metal, so stainless steel, plastic, glass and wood are used. On a small scale simple hand-squeezers can be used to extract juice. Lime cordial requires the juice to be clarified, in order to produce a crystal clear product. Raw juice contains fruit debris and a cloud caused by fruit pectins, so it needs to be racked or allowed to clear, as the crude solid pulp settles. Calcium carbonate is added at this stage which reacts with the fruit pectins and settles with fruit solids. Sodium metabisulphite is added to preserve the juice during racking.

BIGGER OPERATIONS

Limes are usually processed when mature but when the fruit is half-yellow and not fully ripe. The juice is said to have a better flavour than that obtained from fully ripe limes. The distilled oil from unripe fruit is also said to be superior in quality. Only sound fruit can be used. The limes are washed thoroughly with cold water before entering the crusher. The two main types of equipment employed for crushing limes are the roller-crusher or a screw-press expeller. The roller-crusher has triple granite rollers to crush and press out juice and oil. This leaves very little fine pulp present in the raw juice and the juice settles within two or three weeks in storage.

Screw-presses are generally made of stainless steel or bronze and shred the skins. As a result, the raw juice contains more fine pulp after sieving and takes longer to settle. This type of juice is rarely as clear as that obtained from a roller-mill. Higher yields of raw juice are obtainable from the screw-press. Where the juice is to be distilled into lime oil, the screw-press method may be an advantage.

Settling vats are normally wooden and cylindrical, with removable covers on the top, so that they can be closed and sealed when raw juice is settling. Raw juice is fed into the settling vats by gravity or pumping, usually powered electrically.

LEMON AND LIME OIL
Citrus oils are cheaper to produce than many other essential oils because the trees and fruits grow quite easily in the right climate. There is a large amount of oil present in the peel, which can be extracted by cold pressing or by distillation.

LEMON OIL
Lemon oil, *Oleum limonis*, is especially easy to obtain. Prior to the discovery of distillation, essential oils were extracted by pressing. Lemon essential oil is used as a flavouring in the food industry. It is also used in soaps, detergents and perfumes. A thousand lemons yield between 1 and 2 lb of oil. The immature fruit yields less and the quality is inferior. Citron oil is called *cedro* or *huile de cedrat* and is expressed in the same way as lemon oil.

The oil is said to be more fragrant and valuable if obtained by expression than by distillation. In Sicily, Calabria and parts of southern France the '*Essence de Citron distillée*' is prepared by rubbing fresh lemons on a coarse, tin grater, and distilling the grated peel with water. Higher quality '*Essence de Citron au zeste*' is also prepared. This uses a saucer-shaped, pewter dish with a pouring lip at one side and a closed funnel sunk from the middle. Sharp brass pins in the bottom help to rub the peel.

In Sicily the traditional method for extraction was to squeeze large slices of peel against sponges fixed in the hand. The sponges were wrung into an earthen bowl with a spout, in which the oil separated from the watery liquid. The peel is afterwards pickled in brine and sold to manufacturers for candying.

High quality essential oil is also obtained from the lemon flowers. The peel contains 0.4% essential oil. Petigrain oil is an essential oil obtained from the leaves and young twigs of the tree.

LIME OIL
In the West Indies oil derived from the Mexican lime is obtained by three different methods:
- By hand-pressing in a copper bowl studded with spikes, as for lemon oil in Europe. This method is called an écuelle and yields oil of the highest quality but in limited amounts. It is an important flavouring for sweets.
- By machine-pressing. Oil is expressed from the spent half-shells after juice extraction, or simultaneously but with no contact with the juice.
- By distillation from the oily pulp that rises to the top of tanks of lime juice which have been left to settle for two or more weeks. This yields the highest percentage of oil. With terpenes removed, it is used extensively in flavouring soft drinks, confectionery, ice cream, sherbet and other food products. The settled juice is marketed for drinking and the residue can be processed to recover citric acid.

OTHER USES OF LEMONS
- Lemon juice is valued in the home as a stain remover and cleaning agent. (See the later section on cleaning tips.)
- Lemon juice has been used for bleaching freckles and is used in some facial cleansing creams.
- The oil is used in furniture polishes and detergents.
- Lemon oil is used in soaps and shampoos. It is important in perfume blending, especially in colognes.
- Lemon oil has been used to stimulate and redden the skin.
- Citrus oils are used in flea sprays and insecticides.
- Dehydrated peel is fed to cattle.
- As an ingredient in lemonade, it has apparently been

used to keep flowering potted plants fresh. I've heard of lemonade in flower vases, but not in flower pots. It cannot be used on chrysanthemums without turning their leaves brown.
- Lemon tree wood is fine grained and easy to carve.
- Some fish oil capsules have lemon oil added to them.
- A popular school science experiment involves attaching an electrode to the lemon and using it as a battery to power a light or a small motor. (These experiments also work with other fruits and vegetables.)

OTHER USES OF LIME
- In the West Indies, lime juice has been used in the process of dyeing leather and as a skin conditioner and moisturiser.
- Dehydrated peel is fed to cattle.
- In India, powdered dried peel and the sediment remaining after clarifying lime juice are used for cleaning metal.
- Hand-pressed oil is mainly used in the perfume industry.
- In tropical Africa, lime twigs are popular as chewsticks.

OTHER USES OF CITRONS
- Citrons are used in the Jewish festival of Sukkoth. You can read more in the history section.
- In China and Japan people prize the citron for its fragrance. It is a common practice in China to carry a ripe fruit in the hand or place the fruit in a dish on a table to perfume the air of a room.
- Dried fruits can be put with stored clothing to repel moths.
- In southern China, the juice is used to wash fine linen.
- In some of the South Pacific islands, cedrat and petitgrain oil is distilled from the leaves and twigs of citron trees for the French perfume industry.
- The flowers have been distilled for essential oil which has limited use in scent manufacturing.
- The wood is used for walking sticks. In India it is used to make agricultural implements.

Beauty
Treatments

HOME MADE BEAUTY TREATMENTS

I cannot claim to have tried out all of these natural treatments. As always, I include them for interest as much as anything. Always test out new ingredients before applying to the face and avoid contact with lemon or lime juice near the eyes. Lemon is used in face masks for refreshing the skin. Lemon juice is also believed by many to lighten the skin when applied topically, as it has been suggested that the acids it contains inhibit melanin production.

PRECAUTIONS

Because of their concentrated nature, essential oils generally should not be applied directly to the skin in an undiluted form. They should be blended with a vegetable carrier oil or other ingredient before being applied. Common carrier oils include olive, almond and grape seed. Many citrus oils are photosensitisers, meaning that they increase the skin's reaction to sunlight and make it more likely to burn.

When applied to hair, citric acid opens up the outer layer, also known as the cuticle. While the cuticle is open, it allows for a deeper penetration into the hair shaft and so may damage the hair.

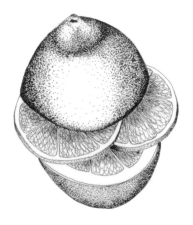

NATURAL INGREDIENT FACIALS

If you are using an ingredient on your skin for the first time, apply a small drop to your inner arm to check for an allergic reaction. Don't use if your arm itches or becomes red.

AVOCADO AND CUCUMBER FACE MASK   92

EGG AND LEMON CLEANSER   90

HEMP SEED FACE POLISH WITH GREEN TEA

    (FOR MEN)   92

LAVENDER LEMON FACIAL TONER   91

LEMON AND CUCUMBER CLEANSER (OILY SKIN)   90

LEMON AND HONEY FACE PACK (DRY SKIN)   88

LEMON AND OAT FACIAL MASK   89

LEMON, HONEY AND STRAWBERRY MASK

    FOR OILY SKIN   89

LEMON-GINGER OATMEAL FACIAL   91

LIME AND GRATED TOMATO CLEANSER   90

LIME JUICE TONER   90

TURMERIC AND FRESH LIME JUICE   90

YOGHURT AND LEMON FACIAL

    FOR NORMAL SKIN   88

LEMON AND HONEY FACE PACK (DRY SKIN)

In case there's anyone not intent on getting a tan and actively wanting to lighten the skin, this face mask may fit the bill. Lemon juice is more effective at lightening than lime juice, I'm told. Just mix enough for one treatment at a time. You can use this on the rest of your body, if you want to.

You will need:
Use equal quantities of lemon or lime juice and honey

Method:
1. Mix the ingredients.
2. Apply to your face and sit down for 10 minutes.

The lemon will rejuvenate your skin and help to maintain the skin's pH balance.

YOGHURT AND LEMON FACIAL FOR NORMAL SKIN

This one combines the astringency of lemon with the cooling qualities of yoghurt. You may need to think ahead for this and have something to put the flour paste into when you remove it. Otherwise, you might block the sink.

You will need:
4 tablespoons flour
4 tablespoons plain yoghurt
1 teaspoon lemon juice

Method:
1. Mix the ingredients together thoroughly to make a paste.
2. Apply the paste to the face with your fingertips, avoiding the eye area. Leave for 15 to 20 minutes before washing off with warm water, followed by cold water. Pat dry with a soft towel.

LEMON, HONEY AND STRAWBERRY MASK
(FOR OILY SKIN)

You will need:
- ½ teaspoon lemon juice
- 1 egg white
- 1 teaspoon honey, warmed slightly
- 2 strawberries, crushed
- 2–3 drops eucalyptus oil or jojoba oil (optional)

Method:
1. Mix the ingredients together and apply to the face and neck. Leave for 10 to 15 minutes before removing carefully and rinsing with warm water.

LEMON AND OAT FACIAL MASK

This is good for oily skin types. Mix and use immediately for best results.

For one face mask you will need:
- 2 tablespoons sour cream
- 1 teaspoon finely powdered oats
- 1 teaspoon freshly squeezed lemon juice
- 1 drop lemon essential oil

Method:
1. Mix the sour cream, oats, lemon juice and oil together in a bowl.
2. Massage over a clean face and neck skin. Leave on for 10 minutes.
3. Rinse well with warm water and follow with toner and moisturiser.

If you are more adventurous you might be interested in some of these:

LEMON AND CUCUMBER CLEANSER (OILY SKIN)

Apply a mixture of equal amounts of lemon and cucumber juice on the face and/or whole body. Leave it for 15 minutes and wash off.

LIME AND GRATED TOMATO CLEANSER

Apply a mixture of 3–4 drops of lime juice and a grated tomato onto the face and neck for 15 minutes. Wash with cold water and repeat daily for two weeks.

TURMERIC AND FRESH LIME JUICE

Make a paste of turmeric powder with fresh lime juice and apply. This will need very careful washing off, otherwise you might look jaundiced.

LIME JUICE TONER

Cut a lime into slices and rub on the face slowly 2–3 times. Leave for about 5 minutes, then wash with cool water.
Repeat 3–4 times a week.

EGG AND LEMON CLEANSER

Squeeze half a lemon and mix the juice with one beaten egg white. Apply on your face and leave for as long as possible.
Wash your face with warm water.

LAVENDER LEMON FACIAL TONER

This is suitable for any skin type and smells fabulous, thanks to the lavender and essential oils.

You will need:
12 tablespoons lavender water
2 tablespoons lavender tincture
½ tablespoon vegetable glycerine
15 drops lemon essential oil
5 drops geranium essential oil
2 drops lemon myrtle essential oil
2 drops ylang ylang essential oil

Method:
1. Mix all the ingredients together.
2. Pour into a glass bottle with a tightly fitting lid. Shake well before using.
3. Apply using cotton wool to a clean face and neck, morning and night. It will help keep your skin fresh and toned. It will keep for a month or two.

LEMON-GINGER OATMEAL FACIAL

The essential oils are cleansing and astringent while the oats are soothing and gentle.

You will need:
2 tablespoons ground oats
1 tablespoon skimmed milk
1 egg white
1 drop ginger essential oil
1 drop lemon essential oil

Method:
1. Combine the buttermilk or skimmed milk and egg white. Stir vigorously.
2. Add to the oats and stir until a smooth paste forms. If the mixture is too runny, add a few more oats to absorb some of the liquid.
3. Add the essential oils and stir.
4. Smooth a layer of the mask over your clean face and

neck, avoiding the eyes. Rest for 10—15 minutes.
5. Rinse well with warm water and pat face and neck dry. Follow with toner and moisturiser.

AVOCADO AND CUCUMBER FACE MASK

You will need:
¼ of a cucumber, peeled and chopped
½ an avocado
3 tablespoons finely powdered oats
3 tablespoons of water
1 tablespoon fresh lemon juice
1 teaspoon honey
8—9 tablespoons green clay or kaolin
Few drops of essential oils (optional)

Method:
1. Purée the cucumber and avocado flesh in a food processor with water and lemon juice until smooth.
2. Add the oats, honey and essential oils.
3. Pour the mix into a bowl and then whisk in the clay. Apply to clean face and neck and leave on for 20—30 minutes.
4. Rinse off with warm water then use a toner and moisturiser.

HEMPSEED FACE POLISH WITH GREEN TEA (FOR MEN)

The hempseed flour contributes a smooth, exfoliating texture with the benefits of essential fatty acids. Green tea is a good antioxidant and oat flour a soothing cleanser. Chickpea flour can be used instead, for convenience.

You will need:
1 cup oat flour
¼ cup hempseed flour (or chickpea flour)
2 green tea bags
15 drops lime essential oil
5 drops cypress essential oil

5 drops lavender essential oil

5 drops juniper berry essential oil

Method:

1. Place the oat flour and hempseed flour in a clean bowl and mix. Break open the green tea bags and add the tea to the flours and mix well.

2. Add the essential oils, one by one, stirring after each.

3. Transfer to a clean air-tight container. Leave the mixture for 3 to 5 days before using.

4. Use a clean spoon to scoop about a quarter of the mixture into the palm of your hand. Mix with enough water, herbal tea or hydrosol to make a smooth paste.

5. Massage gently over face and neck. Rinse well.

OTHER TREATMENTS

APRICOT, LEMON AND

    SUGAR HAND TREATMENT   97

BODY SUGARING   94

FRECKLE LIGHTENER   96

LIME AND GINGER SALT SCRUB

    FOR FEET AND ELBOWS   96

MASSAGE CREAM   98

NAIL AND HAND WHITENING TREATMENT   96

OLD WIVES' REMEDY?   95

REMOVING DARK CIRCLES

    UNDERNEATH THE EYES   98

SALT AND LEMON GOMMAGE   97

SMOOTHING SKIN LOTION   97

BODY SUGARING

This was used by the ancient Egyptians, or so I've heard. Body sugaring is a method for removing body hair that is an alternative to waxing or shaving. I have included it as an interesting alternative, but am not inclined to try this at home! As with waxing, there will be pain involved and heat, so it isn't everyone's cup of tea. I'm assured that it is less painful than waxing, but I'm afraid I'm not going to be a guinea pig for this one. I have painful memories of waxing whilst drinking wine in the past, but we won't go into that now.

The principle involves making a ball of sugary substance and cooling it, before applying to strips of cloth. Then, what a rip off! Proceed with extreme caution, if you must, and try out a small area of leg or arm first.
You will need a sugar thermometer and some strips of cotton fabric.

You will need:

> 450 g (1 lb) sugar
> 4 tablespoons lemon juice
> 4 tablespoons water

Method:

1. Combine the ingredients in a heavy saucepan, and heat slowly. Watch the mixture very carefully so that it doesn't boil over. Heat the mixture to 130°C (250°F) on the thermometer.
2. Remove from the heat and let it cool enough to pour into a bowl or jar. This jar will be reheated in the future. Rip clean cotton fabric into strips.
3. Let the mixture cool so that it won't burn your skin. Test the mixture on the back of your hand.
4. Using a pallet knife or lolly stick, spread the cooled sugar onto your skin. Cover with the cloth strips, let it set for a few minutes, and then rip off quickly. Ow!
5. You can reheat the mixture to a warm (but not hot!) temperature and reuse. Reheating will thicken the paste.

OLD WIVES' REMEDY?

An old remedy for wrinkles was to apply lemon directly to the skin, leave it on for two to three hours and then massage the area with olive oil. Fruit acids are highly valued in the cosmetics industry. Who has got two or three hours to spare? Remember that lemon juice can be a stimulant and redden the skin as well. Some people have very sensitive skin, so try a small area first. Blemishes and age spots can become fainter if you apply lemon juice a few times a day.

FRECKLE LIGHTENER

Why don't people like freckles? I don't know.
My husband and daughter both have so many
freckles that they join together and look like a
suntan! An old suggestion for lightening them is
to use equal parts of lemon juice,
glycerine, olive oil and curdled milk at night.
Yuck. I still like the freckles, myself.

LIME AND GINGER SALT SCRUB
FOR FEET AND ELBOWS

Dry or scaly skin can be rubbed with the peel of a lemon
or lime. Rough elbows can be softened by rubbing the
area with the cut side of a lemon or lime.

You will need:
  1 teaspoon sea salt
  1 teaspoon camellia oil
  1 grated lime rind
  1 teaspoon shredded root ginger

Method:
Mix the ingredients together and scrub onto wet heels,
feet, knees and elbows in gentle, circular motions.

NAIL AND HAND WHITENING TREATMENT

Lemon is good at removing odours from the
hands, for example after peeling onions or
garlic. It is also a stain remover. For the hands,
take the rind of the lemon after the juice has
been squeezed out and rub the fingers and
hands with the remaining pulp.

If you are a gardener like me and forget to put
gloves on sometimes, stains can be removed
from nails and skin by soaking your nails in water
with lemon juice or lemon slices. The lemon acts
as an astringent and will take away stains.

As a point of interest, I also came across a suggestion that using lemon juice on nails three times a day prevents them from cracking or splitting.

APRICOT, LEMON AND SUGAR HAND TREATMENT

Apricot oil is a good moisturiser. The sugar and lemon act to exfoliate and leave clean, soft hands.

Mix 100 g (4 oz) granulated sugar with a few tablespoons of apricot oil and the juice of ½ a lemon or lime. Rub the mixture onto the hands and rinse with warm water.
Apply hand cream afterwards.

SALT AND LEMON GOMMAGE

Mix 30 g (1½ oz) of hard sea salt with 12 drops of lemon essential oil and enough warm water to make an even paste. Put on a massage glove and start massaging your body with the mixture. Pay special attention to your thighs, backside and stomach. Shower off afterwards.

SMOOTHING SKIN LOTION

You will need:
   1 teaspoon honey
   1 teaspoon vegetable oil
   ¼ teaspoon lemon juice

Method:
Mix all the ingredients together. Rub into hands, elbows, heels and any other areas of dry skin. Leave on for 10 minutes. Rinse off with warm water.

MASSAGE CREAM

If the salt massage doesn't appeal, you might like a massage cream made from equal amounts of egg yolk, lemon juice and olive oil.

REMOVING DARK
CIRCLES UNDERNEATH THE EYES

You need to be careful with lemon juice round the eyes, so this suggestion is really for the area underneath only. Applied twice a day, the application of lemon juice on a pad of cotton wool is supposed to remove dark patches. This is said to work on the neck as well. Adding lemon juice to a jar of cleansing pads might do the trick.

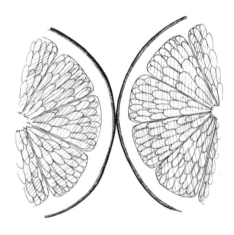

HAIR TREATMENTS

HAIR RINSE   99

BLONDER BLOND   99

DANDRUFFY SCALP   99

LEMON-LIME SPRAY FOR WISPY HAIR   100

HAIR RINSE

After shampooing, treat your hair with a final rinse of water and lemon juice (half a lemon mixed with 500 ml of water) to fight dandruff and sweep out the soap film and excess oils. This might make a nice change from vinegar and smell a bit better. I think that might be better for blonds than brunettes.

BLONDER BLOND

Lemon juice applied to the hair is a natural lightener. A suggestion for blonds who want to be blonder is to mix the juice of one lemon or two limes with some mild shampoo. Massage in and sit in the sun for 20 minutes before rinsing and conditioning, as the juice won't do your hair any favours.

Hair can be lightened or highlighted with lemon juice in a solution with water. Make sure that you have equal quantities, or slightly more lemon juice. Comb through and leave for a while before washing as normal.

DANDRUFFY SCALP

Mix 1 teaspoon lemon juice with 2 teaspoons vinegar and massage into the scalp. Follow this up with a mild shampoo or an egg shampoo.

Another suggestion is to mix 100 ml witch hazel with 1 tablespoon fresh lemon juice in 200 ml water. Shampoo your hair and apply to the scalp when the hair is still wet. Repeat several times until the dandruff is treated.

LEMON-LIME SPRAY FOR WISPY HAIR

Mix 8 tablespoons of water with 1 teaspoon of lemon juice and ¼ teaspoon of lime juice in a spray bottle. Shake the bottle to mix thoroughly and spray onto dry hair to tame flyaways. Keep in the fridge.

Cleaning With Lemons

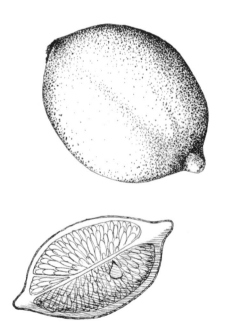

HOME CLEANING USES

The lemon's properties offer a very green alternative to cleaning in the home. The antibacterial qualities mean that it is safe to use in the kitchen and the lovely fresh smell means that it is an ingredient included in many commercially produced cleaners.

Cleaning with natural ingredients like vinegar, bicarbonate of soda and lemon juice is much safer and cheaper than using commercial products. There are so many uses that I've written books on each of these other great cleaning agents. Lemon has the following advantages:

- **IT IS BIODEGRADABLE. LEMON IS A MILD ORGANIC ACID.**

- **IT IS SAFE FOR STAINLESS STEEL AND IS USED IN THE FOOD INDUSTRY.**

- **IT IS SAFE TO HANDLE.**

- **IT DOESN'T LEAVE HARMFUL RESIDUES BEHIND.**

- **IT KILLS SOME BACTERIA.**

- **IT ACTS AS A SHORT-TERM ANTISEPTIC.**

- **IT SMELLS GOOD.**

When you combine the effectiveness of lemon with other substances, like vinegar or bicarbonate of soda, you have quite a powerful workforce to hand. Here are a few suggestions for cleaning with lemons and other natural ingredients.

KITCHEN AND BATHROOM CLEANING JOBS

Lemon juice can be used to dissolve soap scum and hard water deposits. If you are using an ingredient for the first time on an old or valuable item, try it out on a small, inconspicuous area first. Leave for a while and only proceed if all is well. You can use bottled lemon juice for cleaning. The good thing is that, even if the bottled juice is out of date for cooking, it can still be used for cleaning, so don't throw it away.

SINKS
Add lemon juice to bicarbonate of soda to make an excellent stain remover and a safe, mild bleach. Use a couple of tablespoons of each and wipe around the sink. Flush away with hot water.

CLEANING COPPER AND BRASS
Clean copper-bottomed pots and pans with lemon juice. Brass and copper fixtures can also be cleaned with lemon juice. Cut a lemon in half and dip it in some salt. Use to clean spots from handles and other fittings. Rinse after use and dry thoroughly.

Another, perhaps less messy, way is to combine equal parts of lemon juice and white vinegar. Wipe it off with a paper towel and then polish with a soft, dry cloth.

BRASS CLEANER
Another way is to sprinkle some bicarbonate of soda onto half a lemon and rub the item clean. Rinse and polish dry thoroughly. If you don't like the idea of dripping lemon juice everywhere, here's another idea:
> Mix one spoonful of salt with two of bicarbonate of soda. Mix with a little lemon juice. Spread this over the offending article and leave to dry. Rub off with a scouring pad.

CLEANING SAUCEPANS
To get rid of burnt-on food, pour warm water into the pan and add lemon slices. Put onto the heat and let the pot simmer for about 15 minutes. The food should lift off. If not, try using bicarbonate of soda with lemon juice.

WORKTOPS
Try removing worktop stains with a little lemon juice placed on the stain for a few minutes. Wipe clean. If this doesn't do the trick, rub with bicarbonate of soda. Rinse well and don't leave lemon juice on the surfaces for very long.

DRAINS
Does anyone still have waste disposal units? If you have, lemon rinds can be put through to grind up and, at the same time, freshen the drain.

Pour hot water with a little lemon juice down a drain to freshen a sink drain. The lemon will act as a cleaner and remove odour. To cut through grease at the same time, use bicarbonate of soda or washing soda as well.

FRAGRANT SINK CLEANER
Put about four tablespoons of bicarbonate of soda into a bowl with enough liquid soap to make a paste. Add a drop of tea tree oil, two drops of lemon oil and two of orange or lavender oil.

RIDDING YOUR HOUSE OF ANTS
Place a lemon wedge at an entry point for ants that may invade. You can also put some bicarbonate of soda inside the bottom of the door frame to drive them away. Once they get in the house they are a real pain.

CHROME ARTICLES
Rub a cut lemon over the chrome, rinse and buff with a soft cloth. Very good for my kettle, which is constantly on the stove.

CLEANING STAINLESS STEEL TAPS
Don't throw lemon peel away after you have expressed the juice. You can use it to clean the taps and restore their shine.

BATHROOM CLEANER
This can be used for sinks, baths and showers. Mix up 4 teaspoons of baking soda, 8 of vinegar and the juice of half a lemon. Apply with a cloth and get scrubbing. Rinse with cold water.

Stains on porcelain sinks and baths can also be cleaned with alum powder and lemon juice, I'm told. For bad stains, allow the mix to sit overnight and add more lemon juice to scrub clean. Rinse well, as ever.

BATHROOM EXTRACTOR FANS
Remove the gunk and dust that builds up on shower extractors with lemon juice. It will kill germs at the same time. This can also be used on conservatory fans.

CLEANING OUT A KETTLE
Boil a slice of lemon in an electric kettle and leave overnight to clean and freshen the inside.

CLEANING TOOTHBRUSHES
Although it is not a good idea to allow regular, persistent contact of lemon juice on teeth, it can be used to clean toothbrushes. Immerse them in lemon juice, diluted with water and leave for a while.

CLEANING CUTTING BOARDS AND BREADBOARDS
Squeeze lemon juice onto the surface and rub it in. Leave overnight to disinfect and remove stains.

CLEANING GLASS CONTAINERS
Pour lemon juice and water into vases or other objects and add a tablespoon of bicarbonate of soda. Swirl round and use a bottle brush to get to the awkward bits. For tough stains, let the mixture soak for a while before scrubbing.

BONE KNIFE HANDLES
If you have any of these lying around and they have become yellow with age, try rubbing the handles with a cut lemon. Wash and dry immediately. Another suggestion is to combine salt with lemon juice for cleaning hot water marks off bone like ivory, but I leave that up to you.

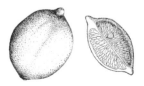

LAUNDRY AND FABRIC CLEANING

WHITER WHITES
Lemon juice acts as a natural bleaching agent. Put neat lemon juice directly onto stains on white linens and clothing and allow them to dry in the sun. Afterwards, wash as usual. You can dilute the lemon in water first if you are unsure about a fabric. For a stronger paste on thicker stains, use the method below.

STAIN REMOVAL
To remove food stains or baby milk on coloured (colour fast) clothing, make a paste with cream of tartar mixed with lemon juice. Spread over the stain and leave for 20 to 30 minutes. Wash as usual afterwards.

Stubborn stains that won't take the hint can be treated afterwards with equal parts of lemon juice and white vinegar, left to soak on the stain for about an hour. Wash the article afterwards to remove all traces of the cleaning mixture.

KEEPING MOTHS AWAY
A lemon in a paper or cloth bag will apparently deter moths from laying eggs and eating your clothes.

If you have the time and patience, you might like to try taking a ripe lemon and making a pomander by sticking whole cloves in the peel. As the lemon dries out slowly the fragrance of lemon and cloves permeates cupboards or drawers. You could even tie it to a hanger or clothes rail with ribbon. There's a nice present idea . . .

OVERNIGHT SOAK
For stained bibs, socks, tee shirts or baby clothes add the juice of two lemons to a bucket of hot water. Soak overnight before washing the next day.

NB DO NOT SOAK NON-COLOURFAST ITEMS TOGETHER, OR SILK ITEMS.

SOAK FOR REMOVING UNDERSTAINS
A speedier soak can be made by using lemon juice with bicarbonate of soda in a bucket. Leave for about an hour before washing as normal.

REFRESHING MUSTY OR RUST-STAINED CLOTHES
If you find clothes that were put away damp, or were left in storage and got a bit wet, they may have mildew stains. Make a paste of lemon juice and salt and rub onto the areas affected. Put the clothes out to dry in the sun. Then all you need is a quick wash and thorough drying. This works well for rust stains as well.

You can also try adding the juice of half a lemon to the washing machine, to boost the cleaning power of non-biological powders.

REMOVING SCORCH MARKS FROM AN IRON
Rub a piece of lemon over the area scorched, leaving as much juice and pith on as possible. Leave to dry in the sun and then wash and dry again. Next time, test the iron first!

OTHER JOBS

AIR FRESHENER FOR THE ROOM
Mix a few drops of your preferred (lemon) oil fragrance with a small bowl of bicarbonate of soda. This is much cheaper than a commercial air freshener, without any cloying or overpowering fragrance. You could even use an ashtray, thereby indicating that smoking is not encouraged in the house!

INK STAINS ON CLOTHES
An effective method in removing ink stains is to use detergent, lemon juice and water. To use this method, apply some detergent to the back of the stain-ridden item. Then, place the item under the cold tap. Rinse thoroughly. If any stains remain, you can treat with equal amounts of lemon juice and salt before washing.

FURNITURE AND WOOD FLOOR POLISH

Mix equal quantities of olive oil and lemon juice. Rub onto furniture, then polish with a dry cloth. This can be used on floors as well. Try out the mix on a hidden part of furniture first. Varnished floors should never be allowed to get too wet, so don't be too generous.

REMOVING MILDEW ON OUTDOOR FABRICS

When lemon juice is applied and left in strong sunlight it can remove mildew from fabrics. If you have to put tents, awnings or canvas deckchairs away damp there's always a risk of mildew. You could try rubbing with fresh lemons cut in half, before washing with soap and water. Rinse thoroughly. That reminds me, my deckchairs need some TLC (Tender Lemon Care).

STAINED LEATHER SHOES

Try pouring lemon juice on a cloth with some cream of tartar and massage into the shoe leather. When the stain is removed, rinse and dry thoroughly, by natural means if possible, then polish the shoes again.

FRAGRANT FIREPLACES

If your lovely log fire is belching out nasty niffs, try throwing lemon or orange peel into the flames. It smells wonderful.

VINEGAR AND LEMON FLOOR CLEANER

Into 2 litres (4 pints) of water, add about 400 ml (16 fluid oz) of white vinegar and 200 ml (8 fluid oz) of lemon juice. Stir well and use on vinyl or tiled floors. On wooden, varnished floors, use only on a dampened cloth so that the wood doesn't get too wet.

PET ODOUR ON A CARPET

To remove the smell after pet messes are cleaned up, apply lemon juice to the area and let it soak for 15 to 30 minutes. Test a small area of carpet first. Once the stain is removed, rinse and blot with kitchen towel. You can also use a mixture of lemon juice and bicarbonate of soda, which also gets rid of nasty smells.

ALL-PURPOSE SPRAY CLEANER

You will need:
- 400 ml (16 fluid oz) warm water
- 2 tablespoons lemon juice
- 1 tablespoon baking soda
- ½ teaspoon dishwashing liquid
- 1 teaspoon borax

Method:
Put all the ingredients into a bottle and use as you would any spray-and-wipe cleaner.

HOME-MADE WASHING UP LIQUID

This sounds good, assuming you can afford the time to prepare it. The ingredients are very similar to some environmentally friendly products which are now available, except for a lack of salt.

You will need:
- 200 ml (8 fluid oz) hot water
- 4 tablespoons soap flakes
- 4 tablespoons glycerine
- ½ teaspoon lemon oil

Method:
Mix the water and soap flakes until the soap dissolves. Leave to cool. Add the glycerine and lemon oil. Stir with a fork to break up the gel. Store in a labelled container until it is needed. Pour 2 to 3 teaspoons under running water for washing dishes.

REMOVING WINE STAINS
Red wine stain can be removed with lemon juice and cream of tartar. Saturate the stain with lemon juice as soon as possible and make a pouch out of the stained area. Pour cream of tartar in the pouch and let this soak. If you can't magically remove the cloth straightaway without disturbing the whole table, pour salt on to soak up the wine and prevent further spread until you can deal with the stain properly.

KEEPING CATS OFF THE GARDEN

Why is it always someone else's cat that likes to use your gravel path or vegetable bed as a glorified cat tray? In our case, it seems to be half the neighbourhood population of moggies, with the pedigree cats being the worst and most persistent offenders! One method is to collect all of your old lemon, lime and orange halves when the juice has been removed. Scatter them around the area. Cats don't like citrus juice. Come to think of it, neither do the slugs. Lemon peel isn't good for the compost heap though, as worms don't like their food garnished.

Cooking With Lemons & Limes

It is difficult to imagine not using lemons when cooking. For me it would be like not using onions or garlic at all. Lemons have so many practical uses as well as enhancing flavour and giving a fresh aroma to dishes. Whether savoury or sweet, food or drinks, lemons are the fruit to turn to.

Limes have taken a bit longer to get on my regular shopping list. I've only recently experimented a bit more with using them to flavour meat and fish dishes, but now I can't think why I didn't, apart from the availability of limes in the supermarkets, as opposed to lemons.

BUYING LEMONS
Buying the bargain net of lemons isn't always cost-effective, unless you are going to use them in a hurry. Because they are so cheap to buy in France, I always end up with more then we can get through, but that doesn't mean they have to be wasted. Lemons that look shrivelled up and past their best are still full of juice, even though the peel isn't very appetising. Even if the fruit is inedible, you can use it for cleaning.

There are other considerations as well. If you want to be sure of buying unwaxed lemons, look carefully at the information, or go for organic lemons. They often cost a bit more, but at least you won't have to worry about chemicals, however harmless they claim to be.

There's often less choice with limes, although some shops stock Mexican and Tahitian limes. As for citrons, I don't think I've seen them in south-east England at all.

Here are some suggestions for keeping lemons fresh and getting the best out of them. Remember though, that fresh lemon juice will not keep very long and if you are using for medical reasons, the lemons should always be freshly prepared to gain the most benefit. For adding a slice to your G and T or for party use, some of these suggestions might be helpful and save time.

- For quantities of zest, to be used in cooking, choose thick-skinned fruit. Wash and dry the fruit, then using the fine side of a hand grater take the rind off. Don't go beyond the outer peel, as the white inner pith is bitter. Store the zest in a small polythene bag closed tightly in the freezer or fridge for a week.

- You can make cubes of lemon juice by expressing the juice into ice cube trays. When you need a small amount of lemon juice, just remove one of two cubes and return the rest to the freezer. If you'll forget which cubes are lemon and which are ice, remove the frozen cubes to a plastic bag which you can label.

- If you only need a small amount of juice, make a hole in the lemon or lime with a toothpick or kebab stick, just large enough to squeeze out the quantity for your needs, without wasting a whole chunk of fruit.

- For garnishing drinks, cut up a lemon or lime and freeze individual half-slices on a tray. When they are frozen, put them in a plastic bag until you need them. You won't need to add ice with your slice as you'll have the two in one!

- Wash lemons or limes under a hot tap before juicing them. They will yield more juice that way. Thinner skinned lemons will probably be best for juicing. To extract the most juice, first roll the lemon on a flat surface to break the inner membranes.

OTHER HINTS AND TIPS FOR USING LEMON

- Use lemon juice to keep fruit like banana and apple from going brown in a fruit salad.

- Avocados also need some lemon to stop them going brown. Always add it to guacamole, especially if it is being prepared ahead of when it will be needed.

- Use it to prevent potatoes and cauliflower turning brown when boiling them.

- Prevent rice grains from sticking together. Add a teaspoonful of lemon to the water when cooking it.

- Keep salads crisp. Salt water may wilt the lettuce, but lemon juice will keep it perky, and kill any bugs or slugs still attached.

- When making jam, always add a teaspoon of lemon juice for added pectin.

- Don't keep ripe lemons next to too much fruit at once, unless you want to ripen it all. Ripe citrus, as well as bananas, tomatoes and a lot of other fruits give off ethylene, which acts as a ripening hormone to other varieties of fruit. On the other hand, if you want to accelerate the ripening of those avocados or plums that never seem to ripen, there's the answer: put them with the lemons and limes.

- Lemons contain acids which are good for tenderising meat. Marinades containing lemon are particularly good for poultry.

DRINKS WITH LEMONS & LIMES

Whether hot or cold, alcoholic or soft drinks, lemons and limes are invaluable for giving a fresh tang. Here are some to try.

SOFT DRINKS AND BEVERAGES

GRANDMOTHER'S LEMONADE CORDIAL	117
HOME-MADE LEMONADE	116
HOT SPICY LEMON AND HONEY DRINK	119
ICED HONEY TEA	118
LIME CORDIAL	117
PARTY PUNCH (ALCOHOL FREE)	123
SANGRITA CHASER	118
SPICED CAMOMILE COOLER	119
TROPICAL JUICE QUENCHER	124

ALCOHOLIC COCKTAILS AND DRINKS

BLOODY MARY	122
GOLDEN MARGARITA	121
HEMINGWAY	122
HONEY RUM STINGER	120
HOT PORT CUP	124
HOT TODDY	123
LEMON MERINGUE COCKTAIL	122
LIME MARGARITA	121

NEW ORLEANS GIN FIZZ   121

SANGRIA   125

VODKA LEMON AND LIME COCKTAIL   120

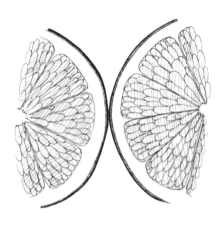

SOFT DRINKS AND BEVERAGES

HOME-MADE LEMONADE

This is how children were given a treat in hot weather in the days before bottles of fizzy drinks were available everywhere. You need to be ready to drink it immediately, as the fizz doesn't last long.

You will need:
- 1 lemon
- 2 tablespoons icing sugar
- 1 teaspoon bicarbonate of soda
- 450 ml (¾ pint) cold water

Method:
1. Cut the lemon in half and squeeze out the juice.
2. Put the icing sugar into a jug with the bicarbonate of soda. Pour in the water and stir well. This will make the solution cloudy, but most of the sugar should dissolve.
3. Quickly pour the lemon juice into the jug and stir again. As soon as the fizzing dies down, pour into glasses and enjoy.

GRANDMOTHER'S LEMONADE CORDIAL

For the more discerning palate you might like to try this recipe, which makes a flat cordial for dilution. The cordial will keep for a couple of weeks in the fridge. If you like, you can dilute the cordial with soda water, to make it fizzy.

You will need:
> 6 lemons
> 1 kg (2 lb) white sugar
> 25 g (1 oz) citric acid
> 1.5 litres (3 pints) boiling water

Method:
1. Grate the rind from three of the lemons and squeeze the juice from all six.
2. In a large, heatproof bowl or saucepan dissolve the sugar and citric acid in the boiling water. Stir in the lemon rind and juice.
3. Allow to cool before bottling or storing in a covered jug.
4. To drink, dilute 1 part of the cordial in 4 parts water.

LIME CORDIAL

This is something else to make with the children.

You will need:
> 40 g (1½ oz) caster sugar
> 3 large limes
> 500 ml (1 pint) boiling water

Method:
1. Take the zest off the limes in long strips. Put them in a heatproof jug with the boiling water and sugar. Stir well and then leave to cool.
2. When cold, take out the zest and squeeze the juice of the limes into the jug. Chill for at least an hour.
3. To serve, pour into tall glasses and dilute to taste with cold water. Garnish with mint leaves (optional).

SANGRITA CHASER

This a spicy and refreshing non-alcoholic chaser made of fresh orange juice, grenadine and chillie piquín or a mix of different chillies. Sangrita owes its name to the Spanish diminutive for 'blood'. Commercially bottled brands are available, but you can make your own. I'm told it goes down well after a shot of tequila (see the trivia section).

You will need:
   1 litre (35 fluid oz) freshly squeezed orange juice
   150 ml–300 ml (5–10 fluid oz) fresh lime juice
   1 tablespoon of grenadine syrup
   1 tablespoon salt
   ¼ tablespoon Chillie piquín (optional)
      or few drops Tabasco sauce

If you want really red sangrita you can add tomato juice as well.

Method:
Mix all of the ingredients together and drink a shot of tequila, followed by a glass of sangrita.

ICED HONEY TEA

You will need: Serves 4
   500 ml (1 pint) boiling water
   4 tea bags
   Juice of ½ lemon
   120 ml (4 fluid oz) honey
   Mint sprigs, optional

Method:
1. Add the boiled water to the tea bags and allow to infuse for 5 minutes.
2. Remove tea bags and add the lemon juice and honey. Stir well.
3. Chill thoroughly and serve over ice cubes in tall glasses. Garnish with mint if desired.

SPICED CAMOMILE COOLER

You can add a tablespoon of orange juice to each glass as a variation.

You will need: Serves 4
    500 ml (1 pint) water
    4 camomile tea bags
    4 cinnamon sticks
    16 whole cloves
    120 ml (4 fluid oz) honey
    110 ml (2 fluid oz) fresh lemon juice
    Orange juice (optional)

Method:
1. Bring the water to the boil in a medium saucepan. Add the tea bags, cinnamon and cloves, and simmer for 5 minutes.
2. Remove the tea bags, cinnamon and cloves and stir in the honey and lemon juice.
3. Chill thoroughly. Pour over ice and garnish with fresh lemon slices.

HOT SPICY LEMON AND HONEY DRINK

Honey and lemon doesn't just have to be drunk when you have a sore throat or a cold. This spiced-up version is good anytime.

You will need: This is enough for 2–3 cups
    500 ml (1 pint) water
    1 teaspoon whole cloves
    ½ cinnamon stick, broken
    1 level teaspoon ground ginger
    1 tablespoon honey, or to taste
    Juice of one lemon

Method:
1. Boil the water in a pan with the cloves and cinnamon for about 5 minutes. Add the ginger and leave to infuse for half an hour.
2. Reheat before use to just below simmering point. Pour

through a tea strainer into a cup, then add the lemon juice and as much honey as you wish.

COCKTAILS

Quantities are based on each cocktail, so 25 ml is equivalent to 1 fluid ounce.

If you have a cocktail shaker that was given to you as a Christmas or birthday present, this could be the time to use it. If not, a jug or screw top jar will do for mixing. Please enjoy alcohol sensibly. Cocktails can be deceptive!

VODKA LEMON AND LIME COCKTAIL

You can make this a longer drink by adding more lemonade.

You will need:
　　1 part vodka
　　½ as much lime juice
　　Lemonade
　　Ice cubes

Method:
Put ice cubes into a glass, add the vodka and lime juice. Top up with lemonade.

HONEY RUM STINGER

You will need:
　　1 part dark rum
　　3 drops Angostura Bitters
　　1 teaspoon honey
　　1 part lime juice
　　Ice

Method:
Mix together and pour over the crushed ice.

GOLDEN MARGARITA

You will need:
> 1 part tequila
> ½ shot Triple Sec/Cointreau
> 2 parts lemon juice
> Salt
> Ice

Method:
Prepare glasses by wetting the rims and standing in salt. Shake the liquids well with the ice, and strain into large cocktail glasses with a salted rim.

LIME MARGARITA

You will need:
> 1 part tequila
> ½ shot Cointreau
> 1 part lime juice (fresh)

Method:
Follow the directions for the Margarita above

NEW ORLEANS GIN FIZZ

You will need:
> 2 parts gin
> ½ teaspoon orange liqueur
> ½ tablespoon cream
> 1 egg white
> Juice of ½ lemon
> Juice of ½ lime
> 1 teaspoon icing sugar
> Soda water
> Ice

Method:
Shake all the ingredients together except the soda water with some of the ice. Strain into highball glasses over two ice cubes. Fill with chilled soda.

HEMINGWAY

You will need:
    1½ parts white rum
    Juice of ½ lime
    ½ tablespoon grapefruit juice
    ½ tablespoon Maraschino liqueur
    Ice

Method:
Shake well with cracked ice. Strain into cocktail glass.

LEMON MERINGUE COCKTAIL

You will need:
    1½ parts vodka
    ¾ part lemon liqueur
    ½ part white creme de cacao
    Ice

Method:
Shake well with ice, strain into a chilled martini glass and serve.

BLOODY MARY

You will need:
    1½ parts vodka
    3 parts tomato juice
    1 dash lemon juice
    ½ tsp Worcestershire sauce
    2–3 drops Tabasco sauce
    1 lime wedge
    Ice
    Salt and pepper

Method:
Shake all ingredients except the lime wedge with ice and strain into a glass over ice cubes. Add salt and pepper to taste. Add the wedge of lime and serve.

HOT TODDY

This traditional drink will pack a punch to any cold or flu symptoms and help you sleep well, too.

You will need:
    1 part whisky
    1 part honey
    1 part lemon juice
    3 parts boiling water

Method:
Stir the honey and lemon juice into the hot water. Allow it to cool slightly before adding the whisky.

PUNCHES

PARTY PUNCH (ALCOHOL FREE)

The first part of this can be prepared well in advance, with just the finishing ingredients to add when your guests have arrived.

A large punch bowl looks really good, but if you haven't got one you can improvise with a couple of large jugs or even a clean washing up bowl or mixing bowl.

You will need: Serves 10—12
    500 ml (1 pint) boiling water
    120 ml (4 fluid oz) honey
    1 litre (2 pints) cranberry juice
    500 ml (1 pint) orange juice
    240 ml (8 fluid oz) lemon juice
    1 litre (2 pints) ginger ale
    Ice cubes
    Lemon or lime slices

Method:
1. Dissolve the honey in the boiling water and leave to chill.
2. In a large bowl combine the juices. Stir in honey mixture. Just before serving add the ginger ale and ice cubes. Garnish with fruit.

TROPICAL JUICE QUENCHER

You could make ice cubes with extra lime juice to add a bit of extra sparkle. Slices of fresh orange and /or limes also look good.

You will need: **Makes 4—6 servings**

    200 ml (7 fluid oz) pineapple juice
    200 ml (7 fluid oz) orange juice
    60 ml (2 fluid oz) lime juice
    60 ml (2 fluid oz) clear honey
    500 ml (1pint) sparkling mineral water

Method:
1. Mix the honey and a small amount of juice together in a jug until the honey is dissolved.
2. Chill until ready to serve. Just before serving, stir in sparkling water and ice (optional).

HOT PORT CUP

This would be a good choice for a Christmas punch.

You will need:

    1 bottle port
    500 ml (1 pint) boiling water
    1 tablespoon brown sugar
    4 tablespoons lemon juice
    Grated peel of 1 lemon
    ½ teaspoon grated nutmeg
    ¼ teaspoon cinnamon
    6 cloves
    Sliced lemon to garnish

Method:
1. Dissolve the sugar in the boiling water and add the lemon juice and spices.
2. Stir in the port and warm to the desired temperature. Don't allow the drink to boil. Serve in heatproof glasses or goblets.

SANGRIA

This is a light, Anglicised version of a refreshing Spanish fruit wine, nothing like the real thing.

You will need:
  1 bottle red wine
  110 ml (4 fluid oz) rum
  1 lemon, sliced
  1 orange, sliced in rounds
  1 lime, sliced
  350 g (12 oz) strawberries, hulled and sliced
  1 apple, cored and sliced
  9 whole cloves
  1 litre fizzy lemon-lime drink

Method:
1. Combine the wine, rum, sliced lemon, apples, lime and strawberries in a bowl or large jug. Push the cloves into the orange slices and add to mixture. Leave to infuse for at least 4 hours in a cool place.
2. Remove the cloves from the orange slices. To serve, pour a tall glass half-full of wine mixture and garnish with a little of the marinated fruit. Fill the rest of the glass with the lemon and lime and stir gently.

SALADS AND STARTERS

AVOCADO AND TOMATO SALAD   126

BASIC VINAIGRETTE DRESSING   127

BEETROOT, AVOCADO AND ORANGE SALAD   129

CEVICHE   133

GREEK MUSHROOMS   132

HERB DRESSING   128

HUMMUS WITH CORIANDER AND PITTA BREAD   130

MARINATED SARDINES   131

SIMPLE LEMON (OR LIME) AND OIL DRESSING   128

SMOKED MACKEREL PATÉ   132

SWEDISH POTATO SALAD   129

YOGHURT AND LEMON DRESSING   128

AVOCADO AND TOMATO SALAD

One of our French friends frequently serves half an avocado as a starter with nothing more than a teaspoon of lemon juice in the centre. Avocados have a delicate flavour that can be hidden altogether by dressings, but as well as keeping the avocado fresh, the lemon juice gives it a bite. Give it a go!

This simple starter can be prepared quickly. Use the balsamic dressing here, or one of the others in this chapter.

You will need: Serves 4—6
   2 large, ripe avocado pears
   4 large ripe tomatoes
You will need for the dressing:
   4 tablespoons olive oil
   1 tablespoon balsamic vinegar
   Salt and freshly ground black pepper
   1 teaspoon English mustard
   1 tablespoon mixed herbs, chives or basil
   Juice of ½ lemon

Method:
1. Halve and stone the avocados and slice thinly. Sprinkle with the lemon juice to prevent discoloration. Thinly slice the tomatoes and arrange with the pears in a dish.
2. Mix the dressing ingredients (not the herbs) in a screw top jar and shake until they have combined. Pour over the fruit, then sprinkle the herbs on top.

BASIC VINAIGRETTE DRESSING

This can be made in advance and stored for later use. The easiest way to combine these ingredients is to place them all into a clean, screw top jar and shake to blend. On removing from the fridge, the dressing may look cloudy. Allow the oil to reach room temperature before shaking again and serving.

You will need:
   60—90 ml (4—6 tablespoons) olive oil, or sunflower oil
   15 ml (1 tablespoon) cider, wine or balsamic vinegar
   15 ml (1 tablespoon) lemon juice
   1 large clove of garlic, crushed
   1 large pinch of mustard
   Salt and pepper

SIMPLE LEMON (OR LIME) AND OIL DRESSING

You will need:

    4 tablespoons olive oil
    1 tablespoon lemon or lime juice
    Black pepper

Method:
Combine in a screw-top jar and shake to mix. Pour over salad.

YOGHURT AND LEMON DRESSING

You will need:

    1 tablespoon lemon juice
    150 ml (5 fluid oz) plain low fat yoghurt
    1 clove garlic
    Pepper

Method:
Combine in a screw-top jar and shake to mix. Pour over salad.

HERB DRESSING

This is more easily combined in a blender, but you can use a sharp knife or herb cutter to good effect as well. You can vary the herbs, but they must be fresh. It goes well with a bean or potato salad.

You will need:

    1 quantity of yoghurt and lemon dressing (above)
    60 ml (2 fluid oz) olive oil
    1 tablespoon fresh mint leaves
    1 tablespoon chives
    1 tablespoon parsley

Method:
Wash and dry the herbs and roughly chop. Place all ingredients in a blender until smooth. Store covered in the fridge until required.

SWEDISH POTATO SALAD

This is another old favourite, especially good for summer buffets or barbecues. Very pink.

You will need: **Serves 6**
    125 g (4 oz) cooked beetroot
    750 g (1½ lb) new potatoes
    1 tablespoon chopped dill
    1 pickled dill cucumber
    5 tablespoons low fat yoghurt
    1 teaspoon lemon juice
    Pepper
    2 tablespoons basic vinaigrette dressing (see page 127)

Method:
1. Wash the potatoes but don't peel or scrape. Cook them in boiling water until tender.
2. Drain the potatoes, cut into small chunks if necessary and mix with the basic vinaigrette dressing while still hot. Leave to cool.
3. Mix the yoghurt and lemon juice together and season with pepper.
4. Put the diced beetroot, potatoes and cucumber with the yoghurt in a salad bowl and mix well. Add the dill and serve.

BEETROOT, AVOCADO AND ORANGE SALAD

Three super foods in one go! You can use grapefruit for this recipe instead, although some people can't eat it because of medication. This looks beautiful and tastes brilliant.

You will need: **Serves 4**
    2 oranges (or 1 grapefruit)
    1 large avocado, diced
    175 g (6 oz) cooked baby beets, sliced
    mixed salad leaves
    1 tablespoon chopped dill

You will need for the dressing:
>   3 tbsp olive oil
>   grated zest and juice of 1 lime
>   grated zest and juice of 1 orange
>   freshly ground black pepper

Method:
1. Make the dressing by combining the ingredients above. Add the beetroot and leave for an hour or two.
2. Prepare the oranges by removing the peel and pith, and slicing horizontally. Cut each slice in half. Place on a plate with the salad leaves and avocado.
3. Spoon over the beetroot and dressing to serve, garnished with dill.

HUMMUS WITH CORIANDER AND PITTA BREAD

This uses tinned chickpeas, so is a good standby version. If the extra garlic for the pitta bread is too much, you can leave it out.

You will need: **Serves 4**
>   1 clove garlic, roughly chopped
>   1 red chilli, seeded and roughly chopped
>   ½ bunch fresh coriander, roughly chopped
>   1 can chickpeas, drained
>   juice of ½ lime
>   2 tablespoons olive oil
>   salt and freshly ground black pepper

You will need for the garlic pitta:
>   3 tablespoons olive oil
>   2 cloves garlic, crushed (optional)
>   1 tablespoon fresh parsley, chopped
>   4 white pitta breads

Method:
1. Blend the garlic, chilli and coriander in a food processor with the chickpeas.
2. Add the lime juice and the oil to make a coarse paste. Season well and put into a serving bowl.
3. Mix together the olive oil, garlic, parsley and

seasoning. Put the pitta breads under a hot grill for about 1 minute until browned. Turn over the bread and cut the softer, upper surface 4–5 times. Don't cut all the way through.

4. Brush with the herb and oil mixture and return to the grill for another minute.

5. Cool the bread, break or chop up and serve with the hummus.

MARINATED SARDINES

If you have the chance to buy really fresh sardines, they are worth a go. They are so much nicer than tinned ones and taste great barbecued. If barbies are off, they can be cooked in an oven or grilled for about 10 minutes.

You will need: **Serves 4**

    450 g (1 lb) fresh sardines
    2 tablespoons oil
    Juice and zest of 1 lemon
    Juice and zest of 1 lime
    1 medium onion, chopped
    Salt and pepper

Method:

1. Clean the fish by removing the entrails and wash thoroughly under running water. Pat dry and place the fish in a shallow bowl.

2. Combine the other ingredients and pour over the fish. Cover and leave for 2 hours before grilling.

GREEK MUSHROOMS

These can be served as a starter or side dish. This dish is ideal to make in advance as it is served cold.

You will need: Serves 4

    350 g (12 oz) firm button mushrooms
    5 tablespoons white wine
    5 tablespoons water
    5 tablespoons olive oil
    Bay leaf
    1 tablespoon chopped onion or shallot
    1 clove garlic, sliced
    Juice of half a lemon
    1 teaspoon thyme
    1 teaspoon fennel seeds
    1 tablespoon chopped coriander
    Salt and pepper

Method:
1. Wipe the mushrooms, but do not peel them. If the mushrooms are small leave them whole, if slightly larger, cut in halves or quarters.
2. Put the remaining ingredients except the coriander into a saucepan. Simmer for 5 minutes.
3. Add the mushrooms and simmer for 5 minutes. Let them cool in the liquid.
4. To serve, place in a bowl and add the chopped coriander.

SMOKED MACKEREL PATÉ

This used to be a regular favourite in our house. Instant starter!

You will need:

    1 fillet smoked mackerel
    80 g (3 oz) low fat cream cheese
    Juice and zest of ½ lemon
    Pepper

Method:
1. Remove the mackerel skin and any bones. Make into flakes and put into a bowl with the lemon and cream cheese.
2. Mix thoroughly with a fork to combine. Add pepper and serve with toast or pitta bread.

CEVICHE

This marinated fish dish originated in South America. You can use a mixture of fish or all one sort. If you use peeled shrimps or prawns as part of the fish, don't marinate them as they become rubbery. Add them just before serving.

You will need for the marinade:
>   500 g (1 lb) fish fillets, diced into small cubes
>   Approx 100 ml (4 fluid oz) fresh lemon/lime juice,
>   to cover the fish
>   ½ teaspoon salt
>   ½ teaspoon dried oregano

You will need for the second marinade:
>   1 tablespoon olive oil
>   ¼ teaspoon white pepper
>   ¼ teaspoon ground cumin

You will also need:
>   1 medium tomato, chopped
>   ½ medium onion, finely chopped
>   1 teaspoon white vinegar
>   1 jalapeno pepper, seeded and chopped
>   1 tablespoon chopped fresh coriander

Method:
1. Mix the marinade and cover the fish. Leave for 2 hours.
2. Drain the juice completely but don't discard. Combine the second group of ingredients and add to the drained fish. Leave to marinate overnight.
3. Pour off most of the lemon or lime juice. Add the remaining ingredients. Toss well and serve on a bed of lettuce with crispy tortilla chips.

MAIN DISHES WITH LEMONS & LIMES

CHICKEN WITH PRESERVED LEMON

    AND OLIVES   135

GARLIC AND LEMON CHICKEN   135

LAMB AND CASHEW BURGERS   136

PORK CHOPS WITH LEMON   138

POTATO WEDGES ROASTED

    WITH GARLIC AND LEMON   138

SALMON PARCELS WITH LIME AND CORIANDER   139

SALMON WITH LIME AND DILL SAUCE   137

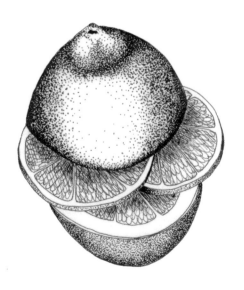

CHICKEN WITH PRESERVED LEMON AND OLIVES

You can use a whole chicken cut into serving pieces or use skinless thighs. The chicken needs to marinate for a while before cooking, so you need to plan ahead. Come to think of it, you need to make the preserved lemons first (see preserves section), so plan well ahead!

You will need: Serves 6—8

> 1 medium sized chicken, jointed and skinned
> 1 onion, sliced
> 2 cloves garlic, crushed
> 3 tablespoons preserved lemon peel
> 2 teaspoons ground cumin
> 1 teaspoon ground ginger
> ½ teaspoon turmeric
> ½ teaspoon ground cinnamon
> Pinch cayenne pepper, to taste
> 2 tins tomatoes, drained and chopped
> 250 ml (8 fluid oz) chicken stock
> 100 g (4 oz) green olives
> Olive oil, for frying
> 3 tablespoons fresh coriander, chopped

Method:
1. Brown the chicken pieces in the oil in a large casserole. Remove the chicken and add the garlic and onions. Fry to brown and add the spices. Stir well.
2. Return the chicken to the pan or dish. Add the chopped tomatoes and chicken stock. Bring to the boil and then simmer gently for 30 minutes.
3. Add the olives and lemon and cook for a further 15 to 20 minutes, reducing the liquid if necessary. Serve with the coriander sprinkled on top and with rice or couscous.

GARLIC AND LEMON CHICKEN

Here's another example of how well lemons go with garlic and chicken. It cooks slowly in the oven. Because the garlic remains in whole cloves, the flavour is subtler and delicious.

You will need: Serves 6

    1 medium chicken, jointed, but with skin left on
    10 cloves garlic, unpeeled
    2 lemons washed and cut into chunks
    2 tablespoons fresh thyme
    3 tablespoons olive oil
    150 ml (5 fluid oz) chicken stock
    Black pepper

Method:
1. Pre-heat the oven to 170°C (325°F, gas mark 3).
2. Put the chicken pieces into a roasting tin with the whole cloves of garlic, oil, lemon chunks and the thyme.
3. Pour over the chicken stock and add black pepper. Cover tightly with foil and put in the oven to cook gently for 2 hours.
4. Turn up the oven to 200°C (400°F, gas mark 6) and remove the foil. Make sure the joints are skin side up and return to the oven for 20 minutes to brown. Yum!

LAMB AND CASHEW BURGERS

These have become a regular favourite for barbecues at our house. They have changed in recipe from, originally, neck of lamb, to ready-bought, minced lamb, but either will do. I've just gone for ease and speed. You need some fat to stop the lamb drying out.

You will need: Serves 4–6

    350 g (12 oz) lean minced lamb
    1 medium onion, roughly chopped
    1 clove garlic, chopped
    100 g (4 oz) unsalted cashew nuts
    ½ bunch fresh coriander
    Juice of ½ lime
    Pepper
    ½ green chilli (optional)
    1 teaspoon ground coriander
    1 teaspoon ground cumin

Method:
1. Put the onion, garlic, chilli, nuts and the fresh coriander into a food processor and chop together.
2. Add the meat, lime juice and spices. Mix until just combined, but so that you can still see some nuts and coriander showing through.
3. Take large tablespoons of the mix and press them into flattened balls with your hands. The size and number you make depend on you. Bigger ones are less likely to fall apart.
4. Put the burgers onto a plate and refrigerate until you are ready to cook. Take the burgers out when you light the barbecue to return to room temperature before cooking.

SALMON WITH LIME AND DILL SAUCE

I used this sauce with a whole roasted salmon for a starter last New Year's Eve. It was very well received and there were, sadly, no leftovers for the next day! The amount of salmon will depend on the number of people, but a smallish salmon served 12 adults as a starter. It would serve 6 for a main dish. Buying a whole salmon (on offer!) is by far the most economical way to do it. Cooking times for the fish will depend on the size and whether whole or filleted. The fish can be served hot or cold.

You will need:
>   I small whole salmon or salmon fillets
>   2 lemons or limes, washed and sliced
>   50 g (2 oz) butter

You will need for the sauce:
>   200 ml (7 fluid oz) low fat crème fraiche
>   Juice and zest of 1 lime
>   1 tablespoon dried dill
>   1 tablespoon capers, chopped

Method:
1. Line a large roasting tin with foil. Arrange the salmon in the tin with the sliced lemons/limes and knobs of butter. Fold over the foil to make a pocket, seal well and

put into a moderate oven, following oven maker's or
supplier's instructions.
2. To make the sauce, combine all of the ingredients and
leave covered in the fridge for the flavours to blend.
3. Arrange the skinned fish on a plate, garnished with
cucumber and lemon or lime wedges. Serve the sauce
separately.

PORK CHOPS WITH LEMON

This recipe is very simple and unusual for me in that it
doesn't use either onions or garlic!

You will need: **Serves 4**
    4 pork loin chops
    2 lemons

Method:
1. Preheat the oven to 200°C (400°F, gas mark 6).
2. Cut the lemons in half. Put the chops on an ovenproof
tray or dish and squeeze the juice over them. Put the
lemons on the tray as well.
3. Roast for about 10 minutes. Turn the chops, pressing the
lemon pieces over the other sides carefully, without burning
or splashing yourself. Return to the oven for another 10
minutes. Baste and serve with any juices in the pan.

POTATO WEDGES ROASTED
WITH GARLIC AND LEMON

Somehow, lemons and garlic go together so well . . .
This has become a regular way of cooking potatoes for us.
You don't need to peel them for this recipe and they
taste much better than chips! They are popular with all
ages.

You will need:
    500 g (1 lb) potatoes, scrubbed but not peeled
    2 cloves garlic, crushed
    2 lemons
    2 tablespoons olive oil

Salt and pepper
4 tablespoons fresh rosemary

Method:
1. Preheat the oven to 200°C (400°F, gas mark 6).
2. Cut the potatoes into wedges and the lemons in half lengthways and then into chunks. Put them all in a bowl with the rosemary and garlic. Squeeze the lemon chunks over the potato wedges.
3. Heat the olive oil in a roasting pan and put all the ingredients in, stirring a little. Roast for 30 minutes, tossing occasionally until they are crispy.

SALMON PARCELS WITH LIME AND CORIANDER

Yes, I know that the ingredients are much the same, but this is another favourite for large numbers or special occasions. The pastry parcels can be prepared ahead of time and cooked at the last minute, as either a starter or main course. If I am making them for a starter I use smaller pieces of fish but the same amount of filling and only half the amount of filo pastry.

You will need: **Serves 4**
    4 x 125 g (4 oz) salmon fillets, skinned
    8 sheets filo pastry
    2 teaspoons grated fresh ginger
    2 tablespoons chopped coriander
    2 spring onions, finely sliced
    50 g (2 oz) butter
    Salt and black pepper
    Finely grated zest and juice of 1 lime

Method:
1. Preheat the oven to 190°C (375°F, gas mark 5).
2. In a small bowl, mix the lime zest, juice, ginger, spring onion and coriander.
3. Melt the butter in a small pan over a low heat. Brush a sheet of filo pastry with a little butter. Place a second sheet over the top and brush this with butter as well. Keep the rest of the pastry covered to stop it drying out and cracking.

4. Put a piece of salmon at one end of the pastry and put a quarter of the contents of the bowl of ginger, lime etc. on top. Fold in the sides to keep the juices in and roll the parcel over until you get to the end. Seal carefully.

5. Repeat with the rest of the pastry to make three more parcels. Brush with any remaining butter and bake for about 20 minutes, until the pastry is brown but not burnt to a crisp. Don't be tempted to pierce the parcel to see if the fish is cooked, or you'll lose the juices. It'll be fine!

DESSERTS

BAKED APPLES   146

FROZEN NECTARINE YOGHURT   149

FRUIT WITH HONEY LIME CREAM DRESSING   146

HONEY AND RASPBERRY ICE CREAM   148

KEY LIME PIE   147

LEMON MERINGUE PIE   149

LEMON SYLLABUB   150

LIME CREAM DRESSING   146

ORANGE AND LEMON SORBET   142

PANCAKES WITH BANANA,

    LEMON AND HONEY FILLING   145

RASPBERRY SORBET   148

SWEET OMELETTES WITH

    LEMON CREAM FILLING   144

TARTE AU CITRON   142

TARTE AUX POMMES   143

ORANGE AND LEMON SORBET

This refreshing sorbet can be made with varying proportions of lemon juice to orange. You can also replace all the orange with lemon. A good way to impress guests or have fun for a party is to wash the fruit carefully and then scoop out the flesh from large oranges or lemons (without squeezing them out of shape). Wash the insides and then freeze the empty skins to get a frosting on before you fill them with sorbet.

Quantities are given in both metric and imperial measures, although these are only equivalent and may vary from one recipe to the next. Use either one or the other, but don't mix the two in any one recipe.

You will need:
  275 ml (½ pint) water
  275 ml (½ pint) orange juice or other juice
  2 teaspoons grated lemon rind
  4 tablespoons lemon juice
  2 teaspoons gelatine or vegetable substitute
  2 egg whites
  175 g (6 oz) sugar

Method:
1. Soak the gelatine in a little water, or follow the instructions on the packet of any substitute.
2. Boil the rest of the water with the sugar for 10 minutes to make a syrup. Cool slightly and stir in the gelatine. Leave to cool.
3. Stir in the juice and rind. Beat the egg whites until stiff but not too dry and add to the mix.
4. Pour into a freezer dish or into individual citrus shells and freeze for at least 3 hours. This sorbet should remain slightly less than hard frozen.

TARTE AU CITRON

This is a classic French dessert. If you want to make it less rich, you can use ordinary shortcrust pastry for the casing and reduce the number of eggs as well.

You will need for the pastry: Serves 6—8
225 g (8 oz) flour
115 g (4 oz) butter
2 dessertspoons icing sugar
1 egg
1 teaspoon vanilla essence
1 tablespoon water

You will need for the filling:
6 eggs, beaten
350 g (12 oz) caster sugar
115 g (4 oz) butter
Zest and juice of 4 lemons
Icing sugar for dusting

Method:

1. Preheat the oven to 200°C (400°F, gas mark 6).
2. Sift the flour into a large bowl and rub in the butter to make fine breadcrumbs. Add the icing sugar, stir in the egg and vanilla.
3. Add enough water to form a dough. Turn out onto a floured board.
4. Grease a 23 cm (9 to 10 inch) flan dish and line with the pastry. Cover the inside with greaseproof paper and add a few dried beans to hold it in place.
5. Bake blind for 10 minutes and then remove the beans and paper.
6. Meanwhile, put the eggs, sugar and butter into a pan over a low heat to dissolve the sugar, add the lemon juice and zest. Continue stirring until the mixture thickens slightly.
7. Turn into the pastry case and return to the oven for about 20 minutes.
8. Cool on a wire tray and dust with icing sugar to serve.

TARTE AUX POMMES

Otherwise known as Normandy apple tart, this apple dish is popular across France. You can use half the quantity of the sweet pastry recipe above, or ready made shortcrust for the base. Although cooking apples are recommended, I use eating varieties from the garden, with less sugar.

You will need: Serves 6
    120 g (4 oz) shortcrust pastry
    1 kg (2 lb) cooking apples
    80 g (3 oz) sugar
    2 tablespoons lemon juice
    2 tablespoons apricot jam, sieved and warmed

Method:
1. Roll out the pastry and line a 20 cm (8 inch) flan ring or tin.
2. Peel, core and slice three-quarters of the apples and cook them with the water and sugar until soft. Mash them to a purée and cool.
3. Peel, core and slice the rest of the apples. Spread the purée in the lined flan tin and then arrange the slices of raw apple in circles to cover the top. Brush with the lemon juice.
4. Bake at 190°C (375°F, gas mark 5) for 25 minutes. Brush with apricot jam as soon as it comes out of the oven. Serve hot or cold.

SWEET OMELETTES WITH LEMON CREAM FILLING

If you don't fancy the idea of sweet omelettes, but like the lemon cream filling, use the filling for pancakes, as given below, but double the quantity.

You will need for the omelettes: Serves 2
    2 eggs, separated
    1 tablespoon caster sugar
    1 tablespoon butter
You will need for the lemon filling:
    Zest and juice of 1 lemon
    100 ml (4 fluid oz) whipping cream
    25 g (1 oz) caster sugar

Method:
1. Beat the egg yolks with the sugar until creamy. Beat the egg whites until stiff.
2. Fold the egg whites into the yolks.
3. Heat the butter in a pan until bubbling. Pour in the egg mixture and spread evenly over the pan. Cook for

about 3 to 4 minutes, then put the pan under a medium hot grill for about 5 minutes. Remove from the heat.
4. Whip the cream and mix with the caster sugar and lemon. Spread the filling onto the omelette, fold in half and serve immediately.

PANCAKES WITH BANANA, LEMON AND HONEY FILLING

If you are anything like me at making pancakes you might be inclined to buy some ready made pancakes to fill. However, the pancakes I produced using this mixture were my best ever! If you are feeling guilty about all the forbidden goodies you've eaten, redress the balance by using wholemeal flour for the pancakes. You can use this basic pancake recipe for any filling of your choice. Here is one idea.

You will need for the pancake batter: Makes 8 pancakes
    125 g (4 oz) plain flour
    1 egg
    300 ml (10 fluid oz) skimmed milk
    1 tablespoon oil
You will need for the filling:
    3 bananas
    Juice and rind of half a lemon
    4 tablespoons honey

Method:
1. Put the flour in a large bowl and make a well in the middle. Add the beaten egg and gradually stir in half the milk and the oil. Beat until smooth and add the rest of the milk.
2. Heat a medium-sized frying pan and add a few drops of oil. Pour in a tablespoon of the batter and tilt the pan to coat the bottom thinly but evenly. Cook until brown and then turn and cook for another 10 seconds. Place on a warmed plate while you make the rest of the pancakes. Mine get better as I cook more.
3. For the filling slice the bananas and put them in a pan with the lemon. Add the honey and warm gently. Spread onto the pancakes, roll them up and serve.

FRUIT WITH HONEY LIME CREAM DRESSING

You will need: Serves 4

    4 tablespoons honey
    2 tablespoons lime juice
    3 oranges, peeled and sliced
    2 bananas, peeled and sliced
    2 apples, cored and cubed
    120 g (4 oz) shredded coconut

Method:
1. Mix the honey with the lime juice and toss the fruit in it.
2. Layer the fruit alternately with coconut in a serving bowl. Top with the lime cream dressing (see below) or whipped cream.

LIME CREAM DRESSING

You will need:

    120 ml (4 fluid oz) whipping cream
    1 teaspoon honey
    1 teaspoon grated lime peel

Method:
Beat the whipping cream until fluffy. Drizzle in the honey and fold in the grated lime peel. Serve at once.

BAKED APPLES

These are easy to prepare, delicious to eat and don't contain any fat – unless you serve them with cream. The lemon juice is an essential element which brings out the other flavours.

You will need: Serves 4

    4 whole cooking apples, cored
    80 g (3 oz) dried figs, dates or raisins
    1 tablespoon honey
    1 tablespoon lemon juice
    4 tablespoons water

Method:
1. Make a cut around the middle of each apple but don't peel them. The peel will help to retain the shape. Place in an ovenproof dish with the water.
2. Push the dried fruit into the centres of the apples and pour in the lemon juice and honey.
3. Bake at 180°C (350°F, gas mark 4) for 45 to 55 minutes, until soft.

KEY LIME PIE

This seems to be a popular American invention. Obviously, it uses limes from the Florida Keys. Being very sweet, it is not really to my taste. You can use the biscuit base, or a short crust pastry case, if you prefer. Key limes are smaller than other limes, so if the limes are larger, you might not need so many.

You will need: **Serves at least 8**

    Juice of 3—4 small limes
    4 teaspoons grated lime zest
    3—4 egg yolks
    1 14 oz can sweetened condensed milk
    11 digestive biscuits
    1 tablespoon granulated sugar
    5 tablespoons unsalted butter, melted

Method:
1. Preheat the oven to 170°C (325°F, gas mark 3).
2. Crush the biscuits with a rolling pin and mix with the melted butter and sugar. Put this in a 22—25 cm (9—10 inch) pan, pressing well into the sides to form a lining. Bake blind for about 15 minutes and then cool.
3. Remove the zest from the limes and then squeeze out the juice. Whisk the egg yolks and lime zest together and then add the condensed milk and lime juice. Whisk to thicken slightly.
4. Pour into the lined dish and bake for 15 minutes, until the centre of the filling is set.
5. Cool and then refrigerate for a couple of hours. Serve with whipped cream and lime slices.

HONEY AND RASPBERRY ICE CREAM

You will need:

    500 g (1 lb) raspberries
    150 ml (5 fluid oz) cream
    150 ml (5 fluid oz) plain yoghurt
    3 egg whites
    2 tablespoons lemon juice
    10 level tablespoons honey
    Pinch of salt

Method:

1. Sieve the raspberries to give a purée and blend with the cream, yoghurt, lemon juice, honey and salt. Put this mix into a shallow plastic container and freeze until firm, but not totally frozen.

2. Return to a bowl and beat until smooth. Whisk the egg whites until stiff and fold into the ice cream. Return to the container and freeze.

RASPBERRY SORBET

Sorbet differs from ice cream in that it is a semi-frozen ice-based dessert, so is much lower in calories than ice cream made with cream or yoghurt.

You will need:

    500 g (1 lb) raspberries
    4 tablespoons honey
    4 tablespoons fresh lime juice, including pulp
    ½ teaspoon grated lime peel
    240 ml (8 fluid oz) water

Method:

1. Purée the raspberries and sieve to remove the pips. Add the remaining ingredients and mix well.

2. Pour into a freezer-safe dish and freeze for 3 to 6 hours or until firm.

3. Transfer the mixture to a bowl. Beat with an electric mixer until slushy but not thawed. Return to the dish and freeze for 2 to 4 hours or until firm.

FROZEN NECTARINE YOGHURT

Make sure the nectarines are really ripe by leaving them in a bowl with the lemon for a couple of days first.

You will need:
>   5 ripe nectarines, peeled and chopped
>   225 ml (8 fluid oz) water
>   4 tablespoons honey
>   2 tablespoons lemon juice
>   1 teaspoon vanilla
>   3 tablespoons apple juice
>   225 ml (8 fluid oz) plain low-fat yoghurt

Method:
1. Put the nectarines, water and honey in a saucepan and cook over medium heat until the nectarines are soft. Purée them in a blender.
2. Stir in the lemon juice, vanilla and apple juice. Chill until cool.
3. Whisk the yoghurt into the nectarine mixture. Pour into a freezable dish and freeze until crystals form around the edges (about 45 minutes). Stir the crystals into the middle of the dish and return to freezer. When lightly frozen through, whip again and refreeze.

LEMON MERINGUE PIE

My friend Sandi gave me this recipe. She makes great lemon meringue pie, in ultra-quick time.

You will need for the pastry:
>   100 g (4 oz) plain flour
>   Pinch of salt
>   25 g (1 oz) margarine
>   25 g (1 oz) lard or vegetable oil
>   1 tablespoon water

You will need for the filling:
>   1 tablespoon cornflour
>   150 ml (5 fluid oz) water or milk
>   25 g (1 oz) sugar
>   2 egg yolks

Juice and rind of 1 lemon
15 g (1 tablespoon) margarine
You will need for the meringue:
2 egg whites
100 g (4 oz) sugar

Method:
1. Preheat the oven to 200°C (400°F, gas mark 6).
2. Sift the flour and salt into a bowl and rub in the fats to a breadcrumb consistency. Mix in enough water to form a dough. Turn out onto a floured board and roll out. Line an 18 cm (7 inch) flan ring or cake tin and bake blind for 10 minutes. Lower the temperature of the oven to 170°C (325°F, gas mark 3).
3. Meanwhile, make the filling. In a saucepan, mix the cornflour with a little of the milk or water to make a paste. Add the remaining liquid and heat to boiling point, stirring all the time. Cook for 2 minutes and then remove from the heat.
4. Add the sugar, margarine, lemon juice and rind. Add the egg yolks and mix thoroughly. Pour this into the pastry case.
5. Make the meringue by whisking the egg whites until stiff. Add half of the sugar and whisk again. Add the remaining sugar, folding it in carefully.
6. Spread the meringue on top of the filling in the case and bake for 25 minutes, until the meringue is crispy and just turning brown. Serve hot or cold.

LEMON SYLLABUB

This is one of those desserts you can make early and then forget about until you want to eat.

You will need: Serves 4
1 large lemon
2 tablespoons brandy
50 g (2 oz) caster sugar
275 ml (10 fluid oz) whipping or double cream
150 ml (5 fluid oz) white wine or sherry
Lemon slices for a garnish

Method:
1. Grate the zest from the rind and squeeze the juice from the lemon. Put into a bowl with the wine, sugar and brandy. Stir well.
2. Whip the cream and fold in the liquids. Spoon into glasses and refrigerate until needed. Garnish with lemon slices.

CAKES AND BISCUITS

BRANDY SNAPS   154

LEMON BISCUITS   155

LEMON CAKE   153

LEMON, YOGHURT AND OATMEAL MUFFINS   152

SODA BREAD   153

LEMON, YOGHURT AND OATMEAL MUFFINS

I can recommend these as tasty, healthy and easy to make. They are perfect for a high fibre, low fat diet. They got the thumbs up in our house, even without the syrup topping.

You will need:
175 g (6 oz) plain flour
120 g (4 oz) rolled oats
50 g (2 oz) granulated sugar
1 teaspoon baking powder
½ teaspoon bicarbonate of soda
Pinch of salt
150 ml (5 fluid oz) plain, low fat yoghurt
1 small egg
2 tablespoons lemon juice
Grated rind of ½ lemon

You will need for the syrup (optional):
25 g (1 oz) granulated sugar
½ fresh lemon rind, grated
1 tablespoon lemon juice

Method:
1. Preheat the oven to 200°C (400°F, gas mark 6).
2. In a large bowl put the rolled oats, granulated sugar, and sift in the flour, baking powder, bicarbonate of soda and salt.
3. In a separate bowl, mix together the yoghurt, egg, lemon juice and rind.
4. Add the wet ingredients to the dry, mixing only until roughly blended.
5. Divide between about 10 paper cases. The mix will look very dry, but this doesn't matter.
6. Bake for 20 minutes, or until cooked.
7. Prepare the syrup by putting the ingredients into a small saucepan. Bring to the boil and leave aside.
8. When the muffins are baked, prick all over with a toothpick and brush the warm syrup on the hot muffins.

SODA BREAD

This is the easiest bread to make. Traditionally it uses buttermilk which gives a distinctive flavour. If, like me, you have trouble getting hold of buttermilk, you can make the milk sour with the addition of lemon juice.

You will need:
  250 g (9 oz) plain flour
  250 g (9 oz) wholemeal flour
  2 teaspoons bicarbonate of soda
  ½ teaspoon salt
  25 g (1 oz) butter, cut in pieces
  450 ml (16 fluid oz) semi-skimmed milk
  Juice of a lemon

Method:
1. Preheat the oven to 220°C (425°F, gas mark 7) and dust a baking sheet with flour.
2. If using milk, pour it into a jug and add the lemon juice. Leave to stand for 15 minutes.
3. Sift the white flour, salt and bicarbonate of soda into a large bowl and add the wholemeal flour.
4. Rub in the butter. Make a well in the centre and gradually pour in the buttermilk or the milk. Combine from the centre with a wooden spoon or your fingers, handling it gently. The dough should be soft but not sloppy. If it gets too wet add a little more flour.
5. Turn onto a floured board and shape it into a flat, round loaf, about 5 cm (2 in) thick.
6. Put the loaf onto the baking sheet and score a deep cross in the top with a floured knife. Bake for 20 to 25 minutes until the bottom of the loaf sounds hollow when tapped. Reduce the heat to 190°C (375°F, gas mark 5) and cook for a further 25 minutes, or until the crust is browned.
7. Transfer to a wire rack and eat while still warm.

LEMON CAKE

My mum used to make this cake regularly, back in the days when we ate cake with tea in the afternoons. Sadly that tradition has gone by the wayside in the cause of healthy eating and diets. I know of some people who used to put lemon scented geranium leaves in the base of the tin to give an added attraction to this cake.

You will need:
> 120 g (4 oz) soft butter or margarine
> 120 g (4 oz) caster sugar
> 120 g (4 oz) self-raising flour
> 2 tablespoons lemon curd
> Juice and zest of 1 lemon
> 2 teaspoons sugar (optional)

Method:
1. Preheat the oven to 180°C (350°F, gas mark 4) and grease and line a small loaf tin.
2. Cream the fat with the sugar, add the beaten eggs and whisk until light and fluffy. Fold in the flour and add the lemon curd and lemon zest.
3. Bake for about 40 minutes and then remove from the tin. Whilst still warm, squeeze the lemon juice over the cake and sprinkle on the extra sugar. Leave to cool before slicing.

BRANDY SNAPS

You will need:
> 50 g (2 oz) butter
> 50 g (2 oz) brown sugar
> 50 g (2 oz) golden syrup
> 50 g (2 oz) plain flour
> 2 pinches mixed spice
> ½ teaspoon ground ginger
> ½ tablespoon lemon juice

Method:
1. Preheat the oven to 170°C (325°F, gas mark 3). Grease 2 baking trays.
2. Put the butter, sugar and syrup into a pan and heat until the butter melts and the sugar dissolves. Leave to cool.
3. Add the flour, mixed spice, ginger and lemon. Stir well.

4. Place teaspoonfulls on the baking trays with room to spread. Bake for about 6 minutes.

5. Leave to cool for a couple of minutes on the tray and then remove the brandy snaps, one at a time. Roll them round the handle of a wooden spoon and leave them to set. You can do this bit with two at a time. Serve with or without whipped cream.

LEMON BISCUITS

You will need:

    50 g (2 oz) caster sugar
    25 g (1 oz) ground almonds
    1 teaspoon lemon zest
    80 g (3 oz) butter
    50 g (2 oz) plain flour
    Icing sugar, to serve

Method:

1. Preheat the oven to 200°C (400°F, gas mark 6). Grease a baking sheet.

2. Melt the butter and then beat in the remaining ingredients. Form into a stiff dough.

3. Cut into rounds. Bake for 10 to 15 minutes. Cool on a wire tray and dust with icing sugar.

PRESERVES AND PICKLES

LEMON AND LIME MARMALADE   158

LEMON CURD   157

LEMON PICKLE   160

LIME PICKLE   159

PEPPER AND CORIANDER RELISH   160

PRESERVED LEMONS   156

In the days of Mrs Beeton there were recipes for all sorts of preserves and pickles that might make your hair curl today. Just reading some of them nowadays makes you realise the lengths some people went to in order to keep fruit and vegetables for winter use. The influence of Britain's involvement in India is clear in Victorian times, with endless curry dishes as well as pickled limes, lemons, mangoes and a whole host of spices which we consider part of the everyday repertoire of flavourings today. I read with slight disbelief the procedures for preserving whole citrus fruits, huge quantities of pickles and marmalades, preserves and sauces that have been superseded by the use of refrigerators, freezers and processed foods. The recipes below have been selected for ease, speed, usefulness and the changing nature of our cooking. Space doesn't permit some of the more bizarre recipes!

PRESERVED LEMONS

Many Middle Eastern dishes use preserved lemons in their ingredients. They can be used to add flavour and aroma to a Moroccan tagine or more traditional casseroles, rice dishes, soups and salads. The outer peel is the part you are going to use, in a variety of dishes. Room temperature lemons provide more juice.

You will need:
>   8 large unwaxed lemons
>   4 tablespoons coarse grained salt

Method:
1. Wash and dry four of the lemons. Cut them into quarters but don't cut all the way through.
2. Pack the salt into the slits. Squash them into a wide necked preserving jar. Cover tightly and leave for a few days, when the salt will draw out the juice. Use the rest of the lemons to squeeze juice into the jar so that the fruit is totally covered. Cover carefully, ensuring that there is no salt around the rim of the jar. Leave for at least a month before using the peel. Once opened, store in the fridge.

LEMON CURD

I've never been a great fan of lemon curd: probably because the shop bought variety was sickly sweet and full of colourings and preservatives. I've just realised, whilst looking in Mrs Beeton's tomes that it was called cheesecake back then. That's solved a riddle going back to my childhood as well; coconut cheesecakes didn't have any cheese in them — just jam. Here are two recipes, one with a lot less sugar than the other for those of us who need to be careful. The sugar helps it to keep longer, but the low sugar version should be used within a week and kept in the fridge, maybe for a lemon meringue pie or lemon tarts. Another way of serving would be to add whipping cream to the lemon curd to make a mousse. The method is the same for both. I'll let your conscience (or diet) decide which you use.

You will need (low-fat/sugar version):
    3 large eggs
    80 ml (3 fluid oz) fresh lemon juice (about 3 lemons)
    1 tablespoon lemon zest
    150 g (5 oz) granulated white sugar
    60 g (2½ oz) butter
Or you will need (full Monty):
    4 lemons, rind and juice
    4 eggs
    110 g (4 oz) butter
    450 g (1 lb) sugar

Method:
1. Grate the rind of the lemons and squeeze out juice. Put a large, heatproof bowl over a pot of simmering water.
2. Put in the sugar, rind and juice, butter and beaten eggs. Whisk together and then stir constantly with a wooden spoon until the mixture becomes thick and coats the back of the spoon. This should take about 10 minutes.
3. Remove from the heat and strain. It will continue to thicken as it cools. Pour into warm sterile jars, cover and seal. Keep refrigerated.

LEMON AND LIME MARMALADE

This marmalade can be made at any time of the year, so you don't have to make a lot at once if you don't want to. Don't throw away the pips or the pith as you prepare the fruit, as the pith contains the pectin which is needed to set the marmalade. Old saucers are needed to test the readiness of the marmalade and to preserve your worktops from damaging drips. If you've never made jam or marmalade before, be assured that jam can give you a very nasty scald and retains its heat for a long time, so be very careful.

You will need: Makes 2—3 jars

    3 large thin-skinned lemons
    3 limes
    650 g (1.5 lb) granulated sugar
    850 ml (1½ pints) water

Method:

1. Wash and dry the lemons and limes thoroughly. Cut the lemons and limes in half and squeeze out the juice on a juicer or squeezer. Put all the juice into a large pan with the water. Keep all the pithy bits separately in a small piece of clean muslin or piece of clean old tea towel.

2. Cut the fruit peel into very thin strips and add to the pan.

3. Tie the pips up in the muslin and place in the pan. You can tie it to the handle with thread, for ease of removal, if you want to. Bring the pan to simmering point and leave to simmer uncovered for about 2 hours, or until the peel is soft.

4. Preheat the oven to 170°C (325°F/gas mark 3) and pour the sugar into a clean roasting tin or ovenproof dish. Warm the sugar for about 10 minutes.

5. Remove the pips and pith package and leave to cool somewhere safe on a plate or saucer. Don't throw it away.

6. Pour in the warmed sugar and stir to dissolve thoroughly. Turn up the heat and squeeze the pip package into the pan to get the pectin out, being careful of the heat. Bring to a fast boil and keep it boiling for 15 minutes.

7. Take the pan off the heat and spoon a little of the

marmalade onto a cold saucer. Put it in the fridge. If it sets immediately and starts to form a skin it is ready. If not, return to the heat for another 5 or 10 minutes and test again.

8. Leave to cool a little for about 20 minutes and then pot into clean, dry, warm jars. Cover with jam papers and label when cold.

LIME PICKLE

This recipe needs planning ahead by about a week so that the limes and salt get to work, as in the preserved lemons recipe. It will keep for a couple of weeks in the fridge, covered.

You will need: **Serves 8**

    4 limes
    1 inch piece root ginger, sliced
    1 tablespoon white vinegar
    10 green chillies, sliced
    2 tablespoons sugar
    1 tablespoon paprika
    1 teaspoon cumin seeds
    2 cloves garlic, minced
    2 teaspoons salt
    2 tablespoons oil

Method:

1. Wash and dry the limes. Cut them into quarters and place them in a wide-necked jar with the salt. Cover and leave for 3 or 4 days, shaking or rotating the jar occasionally.

2. Heat the oil in a pan and cook the ginger. Add the limes and juice from the jar with the vinegar and cook for about 5 minutes, stirring a few times. Add the garlic, chillies and spices and cook for another 3 to 4 minutes.

3. Allow to cool and then store in a jar or covered bowl in the fridge.

LEMON PICKLE

This is a lot quicker, if not so authentic.

You will need:
- 2 teaspoons black mustard seeds
- 2 tablespoons cooking oil
- 1 teaspoon chilli powder
- Pinch of turmeric
- 4 tablespoons white wine vinegar
- 2 lemons

Method:
1. Wash and chop the lemons into small cubes. Remove the seeds.
2. Fry the black mustard seeds in the hot oil. As soon as they begin to pop, lower the heat and add the chilli powder and the vinegar.
3. Stir in the lemon, remove from the heat and leave to cool. Store in the fridge for a week.

PEPPER AND CORIANDER RELISH

I just love fresh coriander and lime together. This is dead easy to make in a food processor and is delicious with barbecue food. Make it fresh earlier in the day and keep it in the fridge until needed.

You will need:
- 4 tablespoons lime juice
- 4 tablespoons fresh coriander
- 2 large tomatoes, skinned and deseeded
- 1 small red onion
- 1 medium green pepper
- 1 fresh green chilli
- Salt and pepper

Method:
Put all of the ingredients into a food processor and chop just until the ingredients are still recognisable, but mushy. Put into a dish and keep in the fridge, covered until required.